Temple Israel

Library

Minneapolis, Minn.

———

    Please sign your full name on the **above** card.

    Return books promptly to the **Library or** Temple Office.

    Fines will be charged for overdue books or for damage or loss of same.

JEWISH ADVENTURES IN AMERICA

The Story of 300 Years of Jewish Life

in the United States

Elma Ehrlich Levinger

DESIGNED BY
WILLIAM STEINEL

BLOCH
PUBLISHING
COMPANY
NEW YORK

A BLOCH CENTENNIAL PUBLICATION
5718 — 1958

to my husband LEE J. LEVINGER
a very patient teacher

a word to the reader

This is the history of the Jew in these United States from the time when New York was still New Amsterdam up to 1954-55 when American Jews celebrate the three hundredth anniversary of the coming of a little band of war refugees.

In a volume of this size it has been impossible to tell the whole fascinating story. For this reason I have tried to highlight my account with the biographies of certain Jews who chanced to play a part in one of the Great Adventures of American Life. So perhaps you may prefer to call this not a history in the usual sense, but a collection of the life stories of a number of Jewish Americans. These Jews have long been my friends and I hope they become yours.

Today, thanks to the research inspired by the Tercentenary, Jewish scholars have unearthed many new and thrilling bits of information. These new facts have been of the greatest value to me in writing these Adventures. Many may read like fiction stories but every tale I tell here is true.

Los Altos, Calif.
December, 1954   **ELMA EHRLICH LEVINGER**

TABLE OF CONTENTS

part one *WE COME TO AMERICA*

part two WE GROW WITH AMERICA

part three WE PAY OUR DEBT TO AMERICA

ILLUSTRATIONS

*Illustrations from filmstrips for the Union of American Hebrew Congregations
by Victor Kayfetz Productions, Inc.

part one

WE COME
TO AMERICA

"A LONG, LONG WAY TO FIND A HOME"

On a September morning in 1654 the citizens of New Amsterdam heard that a ship had just been sighted entering the harbor. Everyone but the bedridden, the very old and the very young, tumbled from their little houses and few shops to hurry down the twisted streets. A ship from Holland might carry letters from home or even a relative come to settle in the tiny but thriving Dutch colony. Or, rejoiced the eager housewives, the vessel might hail from the West Indies and be laden with spice and sugar and coffee. Meanwhile their husbands grinned as they saw themselves gathered in the tavern that evening to listen to the stories the captain and his crew would tell over their brimming mugs.

Today as the burghers strained their eyes to read the letters on the ship's prow, a burly, grizzled man, more learned in seafaring than his neighbors, declared that the vessel had left Brazil many months before.

" 'Tis the St. Charles!" exclaimed the retired sea captain. "From Brazil. A long, hard journey on stormy seas."

New Amsterdam, like New York, as it would soon be re-named, was already the meeting place of men of many nations. Among those who jostled each other in their eagerness for a better view of the passengers on the decks of the St. Charles were Swedes and Poles, Germans and Irish, and even a few

3

Negroes.

Near the old sea captain stood a man sturdy and bearded, his dark skin and hair in strong contrast to the fair, stolid Dutchmen around him. Jacob Barsimson, who had arrived from Holland just a month before, leaned forward eagerly as he caught his first glimpse of the wan, wearied passengers. He had been lonely among strangers in New Amsterdam; it would be good to meet his fellow Jews again!

"It has, indeed, been a long, hard journey," he repeated the captain's words. Barsimson was sure that the man beside him knew nothing of Jewish history; but he could not help adding out of his own knowledge and pity: "Those Hebrews have come a long, long way to find a home."

THE ADVENTURE BEGINS

The great Adventure had really started in Spain. Here the Jews had known a Golden Age of learning and accomplishment; but their happy security had turned into a cruel nightmare for the folk of Israel. A number had been converted and were known as New Christians; some of them secretly returned to Judaism. These Marranos when detected were harshly punished for their backsliding.

It was the year 1492. In the harbor of Palos the crews of three small vessels waited impatiently for their admiral,

4

Christopher Columbus, to give the signal to heave anchor and set out upon the Sea of Darkness. Now he paced the deck of the *Santa Maria,* the flagship of the daring but untried fleet, a broad-shouldered man with a shock of heavy graying hair and a stubborn chin. His eyes, heavy with dreams, scanned the harbor thickly dotted with little boats; many of them seemed unseaworthy to the experienced navigator's eye; all of them were dangerously overcrowded. But more and still more passengers came down to the water's edge to stand and plead for passage.

It is likely that Columbus was too much occupied with his own hopes and fears to pity these desperate Jews driven from Spain into exile in many lands. But the man who leaned over the rail of the *Santa Maria* knew the meaning of the tragedy that spread before him; he tried to hide the tears he shed for the sufferings of his people.

For Luis de Torres was a Marrano. Because he was a scholar and the master of many tongues, Columbus had chosen him to serve as interpreter for the fleet. The admiral hoped to find a shorter route to India; here he would need a skilled linguist to speak for him with the natives. Columbus knew that he could depend on Luis de Torres whom he never suspected of being a Jew. And he remained in ignorance of the fact that one of his pilots, the crew's physician and several sailors were also secret Jews.

For days Luis de Torres had listened to the sorrowful

5

stories of his Jewish friends. Because they steadfastly refused to save themselves and their property by accepting Christianity, even the most prosperous faced bitter poverty. A Jew who owned a flourishing vineyard or a splendid house was forced, as the day of expulsion drew near, to sell it for less than the sum required for his forced voyage to some strange land. Rare tapestries, vessels of gold and silver, precious manuscripts handed down from father to son in happier days, were sold for a few pitiful coins. Few household treasures could be carried by these homeless ones, already burdened with their bundles of food to sustain them on their journey and a few extra garments against the midnight cold. The younger men and half-grown boys carried such necessities; mothers bore their infants in their arms and bade their older daughters to watch the weary toddlers given over to their care. But the oldest men, the honored leaders, were privileged to carry the one treasure the Jews took with them from Spain, the holy Scrolls of the Law.

Luis de Torres, as he watched the unfortunates embark in their frail vessels, wondered when and where their journey would end. He grieved that his people who had for so long considered Spain as their rightful dwelling place, should now be forced to seek new homes. He would have pitied the exiles more could he have known of the horrors of their journey to some distant refuge. Many were shipwrecked and perished at sea; others were betrayed by their greedy captains, who

6

robbed their helpless victims of their few poor belongings and left them to die miserably on some deserted island. Those who escaped these terrors met incredible hardships in the lands where they had hoped to find a resting place.

But Luis de Torres, Marrano, scholar and interpreter to Christopher Columbus, never heard of the years of suffering and seeking for a homeland.

One morning a great and joyful cry rose from the decks of the *Santa Maria* as its crew saw a palm-girt beach smiling under the rising sun. The first boat was lowered to take the admiral ashore; in one hand he held a naked sword, in the other the banners of their Catholic Majesties of Spain. Beside Columbus stood the secret Jew, Luis de Torres. A group of half-naked, red-skinned men stood waiting on the sandy shore. Columbus hoped that these Indians—for, surely this was India!—would understand his interpreter. So it is easy to believe the story that this Spanish Jew was the first of all the crew to set foot on the soil of the Western world.

From the journal Christopher Columbus kept we learn that our Jewish scholar has another claim to distinction. Luis de Torres has the doubtful honor of being the discoverer of tobacco.

It happened in this way: the interpreter and another member of the crew were sent as scouts to search on the island of Cuba for the palace of the Great Khan of Tartary. Luis de Torres carried with him a letter from his Spanish sovereigns to their royal cousin—if he could be found. The letter was never delivered; instead of the imagined splendor of the Khan's palace Luis de Torres reported later that at twelve leagues inland he had come upon a village of fifty houses.

The inhabitants, having still to learn the doubtful civilization carried to them by the Spanish explorers, were cordial but could not converse with the strangers. Luis de Torres seems to have tried all the languages he knew, but in vain. No one seemed able to understand a single word but several interpreted his gestures.

When in pantomime the Marrano asked why they carried lighted brands to kindle the herbs they rolled and thrust between their lips, the Indians answered in the same manner that they enjoyed "drinking smoke."

Luis de Torres noted down this strange habit, which he seems to have connected with the burning of incense, along with descriptions of birds and animals he had encountered on this scouting trip. One very showy fowl so closely resembled the peacock that de Torres immediately gave it the Hebrew name for that bird, *tukki* (turkey).

After further explorations, Luis de Torres settled in Cuba on a tract of land presented to him by a friendly chieftain. Here he ruled the simple Indians like an uncrowned king. In his old age he knew comfort and ease and, best of all, peace. Even if anyone learned that he was a secret Jew he encountered neither hatred nor persecution.

So Luis de Torres, scholar and adventurer, was the first of his people to know security and happiness in the New World. But for the rest of his brethren there stretched many, many weary years of hardship and wandering until they also found a permanent home in America.

WILL SOUTH AMERICA BE THE PROMISED LAND?

After the expulsion from Spain in 1492, many, many Jews sought shelter in the neighboring kingdom of Portugal. But four years later they were driven into exile together with many Portuguese Jews. Those who remained were forcibly converted to Catholicism; as in Spain, many of these converts became secret Jews.

Soon the explorers who followed Columbus repeated his glowing tales of wide and fertile lands beyond the Atlantic. Some Marranos joined the Portuguese colonists who planned to build a new life in the New World. These secret Jews hoped to escape the persecution they had known in their former homes; they soon discovered their mistake. The power of the Church stretched across the ocean. Marranos who felt themselves safe in South America to practise their Judaism, were often imprisoned and sometimes put to death. The scroll which

9

bore the names of the martyrs of the Old World now blazed with the names of the martyrs of the New.

Holland had long suffered from the tyranny of Spain and its church. A century after the expulsion the Dutch, having won their own independence, granted certain rare privileges to refugee Jews from Spain and Portugal, such as freedom of worship and the right to engage in foreign trade. Now in 1631 the Dutch captured Recife from the Portuguese and brought deliverance to the Jewish traders and planters of Brazil's capital city.

The coming of the conquerors meant that the Jews of Brazil might now practise their religion without fear. Marranos who had suffered persecution in other parts of South America hastened to Recife and other Dutch settlements to live openly as Jews. Others came from Holland, Germany and Poland; some from Turkey and even the Barbary states.

Among these immigrants were traders and merchants. A number of Jews raised and refined sugar. Believing that after all their wanderings they had at last found their Promised Land, the homeless people built comfortable and substantial houses for their families. They erected two synagogues for the rapidly growing Jewish community of Recife and brought two famous scholars across the sea to act as their rabbis.

All this was swept away in three short years. The Portuguese sought to recapture Recife. Many Jews, anxious to repay the country which had befriended them, served the Dutch as guerillas and commandos. It was a gallant struggle but in January, 1654 the commander of the Portuguese forces entered Recife.

The Jews of Brazil were ruined by the war; their homes had been destroyed, their plantations laid waste. The Portuguese conquerors were not inclined to grant any favors to those who had so loyally defended Dutch interests. Those who had dared to profess their Judaism could expect no mercy. Once again the servants of the Church sought out heretics; after the mockery of a trial the condemned man faced life-long imprisonment or death at the stake.

The dispossessed Jews, again disappointed in their Promised Land, scattered in every direction. Many sailed to Holland where they felt sure of a friendly welcome; some traders, in spite of the uncertain future, decided to settle in the West Indies. Twenty-three Jewish war refugees took passage on the *St. Charles*, which after four months of danger and uncertainty brought the weary wanderers to New Amsterdam.

A DOUBTFUL WELCOME FROM THE GOVERNOR

There were no adventurers, no gallant soldiers of fortune, among the first Jewish immigrants to the little village on the banks of the Hudson. They came as other strangers of many lands and religions had come before them, as thousands upon thousands would come later, to escape from persecution, to earn their daily bread honestly and with dignity. They were sick with fear; they were poor; they wanted a home.

In the year 1654 Peter Stuyvesant was governor of New Amsterdam. The fiery-tempered, one-legged autocrat was a brave and conscientious man who suffered from violent prejudices. He believed that his countrymen were superior to any nation on earth. He was convinced that if the little Dutch colony were to prosper he must do everything in his power to exclude rival merchants who had the misfortune to be Englishmen or Swedes. As he considered every other religion greatly inferior to his own Dutch Reformed Church he begrudged every privilege enjoyed by such inferior citizens of New Amsterdam as Catholics, Lutherans or Friends.

Of course he hated all Jews. Like many other anti-Semites he did not seem to mind contradicting himself. His first argument against the Jews from Recife ran something like this: in Holland many of the refugees from the Spanish peninsula had proved too successful rivals of native Dutch merchants.

12

Peter Stuyvesant swore a mighty oath that he would protect the rights of the traders against these shrewd foreigners.

In the next breath he protested that the thrifty, hard-working folk of New Amsterdam should not be expected to support Jewish beggars. Hadn't Jacob Barsimson arrived a few months before in debt to the master of the *Peartree* for his passage and his keep during the voyage? And now, yelled the short-tempered official, the captain of the *St. Charles* complained that these ragamuffins from Brazil were penniless and would have to sell their goods at auction to pay the just debts they owed him!

Governor Stuyvesant knew that the government of Holland was the most humane and tolerant in the world. He was certain that his superiors in the home country would refuse to exclude the twenty-three refugees from his colony as business competitors or disbelievers in the doctrines of the Dutch Reformed Church. So in a letter to the West India Company of Amsterdam he stressed what he believed to be an unanswerable accusation against the newcomers.

They were, he dictated furiously to his secretary, absolutely penniless. They depended on the kind-hearted pastor of the Dutch Reformed Church for a slice of bread to quiet their hunger, a cup of milk for their crying children. Winter was coming on. It was not a pleasant prospect to have to clothe and shelter and feed these strangers with the funds collected for the local poor.

13

Unfortunately for the passengers of the *St. Charles,* the governor had not exaggerated when he accused them of being absolutely dependent on public charity. Uprooted by the war, even the most prosperous among them had not been able to rescue anything of value. The little the refugees had managed to salvage had paid for their passage. Now the captain of the *St. Charles* insisted that his passengers still owed him a considerable sum. Governor Stuyvesant was willing to oblige him and threw two of the unfortunates into prison, threatening they would remain there until their debts were paid.

Where should the homeless, penniless twenty-three men, women and children, strangers in a strange and unfriendly land, turn for help?

Jacob Barsimson, who considered himself lucky to supply his own modest wants, had lately come from Amsterdam. He reminded his distracted brethren that many of the Jews of Holland had prospered and might be of great assistance.

The unfortunates again dared to hope. When, they asked each other, had a wealthy Jew refused to aid those in want? And the brethren who had successfully established themselves in Holland might aid with their influence as well as their gold! The Jewish members of the West India Company back in Amsterdam might be most helpful in overcoming Peter Stuyvesant's unfriendliness.

Although the unhappy refugees feared the excitable governor might at any moment decide to drive them from the

14

colony, they comforted themselves with the thought that he was not the only one in New Amsterdam who could write letters. The very next ship which sailed for Holland carried a plea to the Jewish community in Amsterdam to help their travel-weary brothers to settle in the village on the Hudson.

The Dutch Jews immediately urged the Directors of the West India Company to consider the prayers of the refugees to remain in New Amsterdam. It was pointed out that the newcomers had been beggared by the fortunes of war but would shortly be able to support themselves.

The Directors proved themselves shrewder business men than the impulsive Governor Stuyvesant. They knew how quickly the Jews who had fled to Holland had established themselves; they knew also that a growing colony must depend on able traders for its prosperity.

For six long months the Jews who had come to New Amsterdam waited and prayed. Would they be forced to sail again on the wide, unfriendly sea? Would they be driven into the dreadful wilderness beyond the colony's protecting wall?

At last the long awaited letter from the West India Company arrived. The Directors warned the refugees that they must not depend on the community of New Amsterdam to support them. But if they were able to care for the unfortunates among their people, they would be permitted to remain in the colony.

The little band of wanderers rejoiced that at last they had found a home.

Peter Stuyvesant was a poor loser. If he could not drive the hated Jews out of his colony, he decided, at least he could make them wish they had never come there to live. Although the West India Company had given the Jews permission "to travel and trade" throughout the colony, the governor forbade them to barter with the Indians who lived along the Hudson and Delaware Rivers. He also refused to allow a Jew to buy a house for himself and his family.

Again Peter Stuyvesant and the "yes-men" of his Council were overruled by the West India Company. The Directors decided that the Jews of New Amsterdam should be allowed to trade and to own real estate. But they were not ready to grant these Jews of the New World certain privileges their co-religionists enjoyed in Holland. Jewish merchants were not permitted to open retail shops in the colony; no Jewish craftsman might practise his trade. Another dear, long-wished-for boon was denied; it was not permitted to erect a synagogue for public worship. But when these sons of Israel recalled the terrors their fathers had known under Spanish and Portuguese rule, they rejoiced that in their new home they might at least conduct private services in safety.

One of the most galling of Governor Stuyvesant's restrictions was the special tax he levied upon the Jews to pay for their release from military service. It seemed to give him pleasure to shame these newcomers by not permitting them to do their share with the other men of the colony in their defense against the Indians.

This was too much for Asser Levy, our first American defender of Jewish rights. At first he found it difficult to pay the tax; later his income as a butcher made payment easier. But he resented as an insult the colony's refusal to allow Jews to do their part in protecting their homes and their families.

"It is my right!" declared Asser Levy, and his fellow Jews agreed with him. "If we are burghers of New Amsterdam we share the burghers' obligation to bear arms in defense of our colony."

The Council of New Amsterdam listened to his petition and grudgingly granted Asser Levy and Jacob Barsimson the right to bear arms like any other able-bodied burgher. But later the local court refused to recognize the Jews as citizens. Asser Levy and several other bold spirits continued the fight. They knew they were building for the future freedom of their children.

A CHANGE OF NAME AND A CHANGE OF GOVERNMENT

In 1664, just ten years after the arrival of the first Jews on the continent of North America, the citizens of New Amsterdam hurried down to the harbor to watch the arrival of ships which brought neither news of Holland nor spices of the Indies. A messenger in English regimentals presented a letter to Governor Stuyvesant which stated that King Charles II demanded the colony's surrender. The letter added that if the governor surrendered peacefully, the Dutch could under English rule keep their land and houses. But if they refused—

Peter Stuyvesant stamped his wooden leg and swore he would never surrender to England. But the more cool-headed citizens of New Amsterdam decided they would be no match for the English visitors and ran up the white flag. King Charles II, who had the habit of giving away what did not belong to him, had already promised the colony of New Amsterdam to his younger brother, James, Duke of York. So word came from England that the colony would be named New York in honor of its new owner.

The Jews who had once suffered from the tyranny of the deposed Governor Stuyvesant had little by little gained new liberties. Under English rule they began to enjoy a freer life. Before long they received permission to erect a synagogue; they rejoiced that they might again worship their fathers' God openly and proudly before all men.

In fighting for their own liberties these Jews had done more than benefit their own people. For every privilege they acquired was shared by other minority groups and helped to pave the way for the equality of all citizens in the thirteen colonies along the Atlantic seaboard.

But this lay far ahead in the cloudy future! Meanwhile Jewish immigrants who had once been repelled by the restrictions of the Dutch rulers hastened to settle in New York. In the very early days the newcomers had sailed from Holland or its South American possessions and were of Portuguese or Spanish descent. In their first little cemetery, which still exists among the shadows of the tenements of lower New York City, the crumbling tombstones bear along with their Hebrew inscriptions the names in Spanish of proud Sephardic families.

For many years these Sephardic families set the pattern for Jewish life in the New World. We see their influence even today in the ritual practised by Shearith Israel, New York's oldest congregation.

It is surprising that the influence of the Sephardim continued for they soon became a minority in the rapidly increasing group of Jews who settled in New York. These newcomers were called Ashkenazim for they had journeyed from several countries in Central Europe, chiefly Germany and Poland. After the English had taken over the colony, a number of Jews arrived there from London.

Little by little Sephardim and Ashkenazim, Portuguese and Pole, mingled and became a confident, self-respecting group—the nucleus of what was to be one day the greatest Jewish community in the whole world.

THE JEWS GROW WITH THE GROWING COLONIES

In one respect the story of the New Amsterdam Jews sets the pattern for the reception of their brethren in nearly all of the thirteen colonies. In most cases they were welcomed with discriminatory laws which, as the years passed, usually softened and sometimes were allowed to lapse. If we are shocked by what seems to be harshness and intolerance, we must remember that the period before the Declaration of Independence was a time of harshness and intolerance.

It cannot be repeated too often that the Jew of that day was not the only victim of bigotry and discrimination. Catholic colonists hated and feared Protestants; Protestants in turn hated and feared Catholics. Both had nothing but contempt for the Friends, mockingly called Quakers. These God-fearing and peaceful folk were actually jailed or flogged through the towns on their return after a sentence of banishment. It is hard to understand, but many people who had left their native lands that they might practise their religion undisturbed in the New World persecuted others for loyalty to their own church.

In colonial America it was taken for granted that the Jew should not have equal rights with believing Christians. It was his own fault, argued the lawmakers, if he could not hold public office or testify in a law court. When an oath was required, ran the accusation, these stiff-necked Hebrews could not expect to testify, since they refused to swear on the New Testament. In some colonies citizenship was granted to any man who accepted the divinity of Jesus Christ—which the Jew refused to do. So the infidels had only themselves to blame.

Yet the Jews in spite of a doubtful welcome continued to migrate to America. They were to find in every colony a group of Europeans who had brought their own ideas and pet prejudices from their former homes. But since there were no "real Americans" except the savage Indians, these newcomers had to learn to live with each other and to tolerate the differences they found in their neighbors.

The Jews who came to the colonies in the early days also had to learn a new way of living in a new land. They learned to share the dangers on the frontier, the privations of pioneer life. Grateful for a haven after many wanderings, they gladly aided in the task of building a new country.

Little by little the Jews throughout the colonies increased in number. As the colonies grew and prospered the Jews grew with them.

TWO MERCHANTS OF NEWPORT

It is not certain just when the first Jews settled in the colony of Rhode Island. Some historians believe they came to Newport just four years after the refugees from Brazil reached New

Amsterdam. But the first actual proof of a Jewish group living in Newport is found in records of the purchase of a Jewish cemetery in 1677.

The founder of Rhode Island, Roger Williams, was one of the very few colonial leaders to grant to others what he demanded for himself. The Puritans had crossed the sea to find a refuge in Massachusetts where they might worship God according to their conscience. But when Roger Williams and others dared to express their own beliefs, the rulers of the Massachusetts colony drove them out into the wilderness. This generous-hearted Congregationalist minister believed that God had led him safely through all his perils; he called the city he founded Providence and promised that it would be a safe dwelling place for men of every religion.

But Roger Williams was far ahead of his time. There was no actual persecution of anyone who wished to settle in Rhode Island. But it was many, many years before the Jewish merchants, who helped so much in making Newport a commercial center, were admitted to full citizenship.

In 1759 the Jews of Newport laid the cornerstones of their synagogue, today the most famous and the oldest place of Jewish worship in this country. The tiny community had appealed for help to the now thriving congregation of Shearith Israel of New York City. The older and wealthier synagogue responded not only with a donation but the loan of a Sefer Torah. Jews scattered through the colonies as well as those of Newport gave generous support. One of the cornerstones was placed by Mr. Aaron Lopez, a merchant of Newport, whom we shall get to know more intimately in a few minutes.

It is fortunate not only for Jews, who are proud of their history, but for all lovers of beauty that time has spared this lovely building; it has long been famous as one of the purest examples of colonial architecture in the United States. Today it is known as the Touro Synagogue, thus keeping alive one of the most beloved names in Newport's history. That it may always be cherished and protected it was recently declared a national historic shrine.

Newport may also claim one of the oldest Jewish cemeteries in the United States. Here again we find many Spanish and Portuguese names on the crumbling tombstones. Many, as

The Touro Synagogue

Longfellow described their flight from the Inquisition, came "o'er the sea—that desert desolate" from Holland and the West Indies.

One of these wanderers, Jacob Rodriguez Rivera, built up his fortune in the whaling industry. In colonial times candles were an important item in every day living; Rivera is thought to have discovered a method for manufacturing the best candles on the market by using ingredients obtained from sperm whales. This president of Newport's synagogue was also active in shipping and importing. Like many of his co-religionists he benefited in his foreign trade from his knowledge of many tongues and was fortunate enough to have relatives and trusted friends in the West Indies who were able to cooperate in his commercial ventures.

Mr. Rivera was prominent not only in Jewish circles but in the general community. He was respected for his princely generosity toward such public causes as the Redwood Library but even more for his sterling honesty. His friends were proud to tell how after Jacob Rivera suffered heavy business losses, he paid every debt to the last penny, although this was more than the law required.

But his son-in-law was even more prominent among the merchants of Newport. Aaron Lopez had been forced to spend his youth in Portugal as a secret Jew. As a boy he may have watched the last sufferings of a fellow Marrano condemned to die at the stake. When he heard that an older relative had settled in Newport, young Lopez vowed to follow him to freedom. In his twenty-first year he was fortunate enough to escape from the land of his birth. He reached Newport and for the first time in his fear-shadowed life dared to live openly as a Jew.

The young merchant bought much of his goods from merchants across the sea; but he also made many purchases from Jewish New York business men whose shops had grown with the growth of the city. His wealth grew with the years; at the time of the Revolution he was master of thirty ships which sailed to England, to Holland, to Portugal. Some of his trading vessels sailed south of the equator; others followed the whales which churned through the cold, far waters of northern seas.

Like many prominent merchants of his day, Aaron Lopez engaged in the slave trade. His sailing vessels carried a full cargo, usually rum to Africa. With this rum or the goods they received for it, Lopez's captains bought slaves. These unhappy captives were shipped to the West Indies where they were sold for cash or native products like molasses. The molasses was brought home to Newport's distilleries to be turned into rum. And very often this rum was sent to Africa to be used to purchase more slaves.

Mr. Lopez seems to have been a generous and humane man, but there is no record of his pity for the hopeless black prisoners who helped to build his fortune. Rhode Island was the most actively engaged of all the Northern colonies in the slave trade; Aaron Lopez, like practically all the merchants of his time, saw no reason for condemning it.

He was among the first of his co-religionists to apply for full citizenship under the laws then existing in Rhode Island. When this right was denied he asked for and obtained the status of a citizen in the neighboring colony of Massachusetts.

Lopez gained many friends throughout New England not only for his business integrity but for his public spirit and what the Rev. Ezra Stiles described as "an agreeable and unaffected politeness of manners." The minister was impressed by the merchant prince's generosity which prompted him to found Leicester Academy and become one of the chief supporters of the famous Redwood Library.

We refuse to leave Newport and its Jews without telling you a little more about the Rev. Ezra Stiles. We Jews should be most grateful to this Christian scholar since we depend on his diary for most of the information of our people in early Newport. The gentleman seems to have been free of many of the prejudices of his day, for during his twenty years ministry in Newport he made a number of warm friends among the Jews of that city.

Every visiting rabbi and Hebrew scholar was invited to Mr. Stiles' home for a long talk on Jewish beliefs and Jewish religious customs. No matter what was his native language, if the stranger knew Hebrew he was sure to enjoy a lengthy conversation with the minister. For he not only knew the language of the Old Testament but he loved and reverenced it. Once he rebuked some of his students who declared that they found the difficult tongue very disagreeable. He told them that the Hebrew psalms "would be the first we should hear sung in heaven, and that he would be ashamed that any one of his pupils should be entirely ignorant of that holy language."

Rabbi Raphael Karigal   Ezra Stiles

This learned Christian grieved when he was forced to bid farewell to the famous Sephardic rabbi, Isaac Haim Carigal. Rabbi Carigal had come to this country to collect money for the poor Jews in Palestine, especially those in Hebron, his birthplace. After he left Newport the rabbi began a correspondence with the minister which lasted until his death. The Rev. Mr. Stiles was then president of Yale. At his request a number of Newport Jews presented to the college the rabbi's portrait done in oils; the worthy minister offered to pay for the frame.

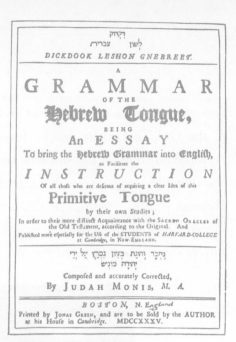

דִּקְדּוּק
לְשׁוֹן עֶבְרִית
DICKDOOK LESHON GNEBREET.

A

GRAMMAR
OF THE
𝕳𝖊𝖇𝖗𝖊𝖜 𝕿𝖔𝖓𝖌𝖚𝖊,
BEING
An ESSAY
To bring the 𝕳𝖊𝖇𝖗𝖊𝖜 𝕲𝖗𝖆𝖒𝖒𝖆𝖗 into 𝕰𝖓𝖌𝖑𝖎𝖘𝖍,
to Facilitate the
INSTRUCTION
Of all thoſe who are deſirous of acquiring a clear Idea of this
Primitive Tongue
by their own Studies ;
In order to their more diſtinct Acquaintance with the SACRED ORACLES of
the Old Teſtament, according to the Original. And
Publiſhed more eſpecially for the Uſe of the STUDENTS of HARVARD-COLLEGE
at Cambridge, in NEW-ENGLAND.

נֶחְבַּר וְהֻגַּהּ בְּעִיּוּן נִמְרָץ עַל יְדֵי
יְהוּדָה כּוֹנִשׁ

Compoſed and accurately Corrected,
By JUDAH MONIS, M. A.

BOSTON, N. England
Printed by JONAS GREEN, and are to be Sold by the AUTHOR
at his Houſe in Cambridge. MDCCXXXV.

THE MOST FAMOUS JEW IN EARLY MASSACHUSETTS

The Puritans have often been accused of intolerance, yet those who built up the colonies of Massachusetts and Connecticut displayed a liberalism far ahead of their day by granting the rights of citizenship to Aaron Lopez and other Jews. In spite of this friendly attitude we have no record of Jews as permanent residents of Massachusetts before the Revolutionary War, except a certain writer and scholar who hardly deserves to be considered a Jew at all!

Judah Monis came to Boston from Jamaica. At that time most of the students at Harvard, the little college in nearby Cambridge, were young men preparing for the ministry. Of course, they all studied Hebrew; for no minister's education was considered complete without some knowledge of the holy tongue. It is hard to believe, but no student was allowed to graduate until he knew enough Hebrew to read and translate the Books of Moses.

Judah Monis easily impressed certain Harvard professors with his Hebrew scholarship. He wrote a Hebrew grammar, a most useful book for teaching the subject; when it appeared it was the first Hebrew book printed in the New World. Later the author gained another distinction. He became a Christian convert. It might have been recognition of this act, or because they thought he should be rewarded for his excellent grammar that prompted a group of Christian clergymen to bring his name before the trustees of Harvard College. These gentlemen promptly granted Monis the degree of Master of Arts.

So now he was distinguished not only as the author of the first Hebrew book published in this country. He became the first Jew—if you can call him one!—to receive a degree from any American college.

Armed with his degree he was considered worthy of an appointment to teach Hebrew at Harvard. Another first! He now became the first Jew to teach in any American college. His classes were large, so his grammar had a large sale but he did not seem to get along very well on the money he received from his text book and his teacher's salary. He seems to have found it necessary to add to his income and opened a shop where he sold hardware, tobacco and snuff. It has been hinted that some of his lazy students found his classes dull; we can well believe they preferred his tobacco to his Hebrew.

Old records tell us that in the early days of the Connecticut colony Jews were given permission to live temporarily in Hartford. Note the word "temporarily"! It suggests the insecurity of our people since such permission might be withdrawn at any time for the most far-fetched reason, or for no reason at all. Jews did travel as peddlers from one Connecticut river town to the next. But it was not until after 1750 that historians discovered several Jewish families in the smaller Connecticut settlements.

In the summer of 1722 a Jewish family—said to have come from Venice!—held "the first Jewish worship in New Haven." They were "the first real Jews" to settle in that college town, the Rev. Ezra Stiles, then president of Yale, informs us. He makes it very clear that he does not approve of the Pinto brothers, who had "renounced Judaism and all religion." Probably an exaggeration; it is likely the family had adopted the churchless creed of Deism, highly approved by both Jefferson and Franklin. But although the Pinto family had deserted its ancestral faith, the sons later took their places in the foremost ranks to fight for liberty for men of every creed and even for those who failed to profess any religion.

PENNSYLVANIA, THE COLONY OF BROTHERLY LOVE

It is very pleasant when studying a period of oppression and intolerance to turn to the story of William Penn, the gentle-hearted Quaker. He truly deserved the proper name of his sect for he was a Friend to all men of every race and creed. Under the spell of his kindness the Indians seemed to forget the trickery of the white men which had robbed them of their hunting grounds. In Pennsylvania in its early days there were no massacres or savage reprisals. William Penn's religion would not permit him to take an oath. He could not swear to keep the pact which he made with his red neighbors. Never sworn to, this treaty was never broken—to the great astonishment of the other colonials.

As a Quaker, Penn knew only too well the persecution which had followed his people from England to the New World. He resolved that in the great forest tract he had purchased from the English king there would always be a welcome for all good men, no matter what their religious beliefs might be. Pennsylvania granted equal rights not only to Englishmen, even if they did not belong to the Society of Friends, but to many religious refugees who came from Germany. The founder extended his tolerance even to Jews.

Unfortunately those who governed Pennsylvania after its gentle founder's death were willing to accept the decree from England that only Christians might hold office or be allowed to vote. But even with these restrictions the Jews found living secure and pleasant in Pennsylvania. A few Spanish and German Jews came to live in Philadelphia, among them several merchant princes of the Gratz and Franks families. The history of these first Jews in the peaceful, tree-shaded city in at least two features is a duplication of Jewish settlement in colony after colony. They acquired a tiny cemetery; some years later when the Jewish community had grown in size and wealth they erected a synagogue. But happily in Philadelphia such steps met no opposition from citizens of the dominant religion. For it had been well-named, the City of Brotherly Love.

A JEW OF LANCASTER

A small number of Jews travelled past Philadelphia and settled in what was then considered frontier territory around Easton and Lancaster. Joseph Simon, whom we have made the hero of this Western Adventure, came to Lancaster in 1735. He was one of the first two Jews in that vicinity to be naturalized and in spite of his staunch devotion to his people seems from the first to have lived in closest friendship with his Gentile neighbors.

He began his exciting business career as a shopkeeper. But running a general store in quiet little Lancaster was hardly lively enough for a man as enterprising as Joseph Simon. He branched out by entering what was then known as the "Indian trade," gradually enlarging his business interests until, we are told, "he became one of the most prominent Indian traders and merchants, and one óf the largest land-holders in Pennsylvania."

His business partners included members of the Franks and Gratz families of Philadelphia. These far-seeing merchants did more than build up fortunes for themselves. Their representatives travelled across the borders of Pennsylvania to Ohio and Illinois and even to the Mississippi River. And in bartering for furs with the trappers and Indians of the Western wilderness, these traders later made the untravelled roads a little easier for the pioneers with their families and their household goods.

From Simon's headquarters at Fort Pitt these lithe, hard-muscled men of the forest followed the twisted Indian trails. At first they carried shining trinkets, hatchets and calico in bright colors to attract the Indians. Later as the cabins of a few intrepid souls began to rise in the forests, the traders carried thread and needles for the housewife and such barely remembered luxuries as tea and sugar. These lonely women welcomed most of all the tiny packets of drugs; they might snatch a loved one from death in a wilderness where no doctor ever came.

33

"TEMPLE ISRAEL"

Over a meal of fresh-cooked venison the trader would charm the pioneer family with tales of the world they had left behind. As he told of his last visit to Philadelphia, a little child, thumb in mouth, might creep from the shelter of his mother's billowy skirts to stare at the stranger. Beside his father the toddler had never seen a white man before.

Back home in Lancaster, Joseph Simon established a synagogue. There is no record of a separate building. But on the holy days when the town's Jewish traders returned from their wanderings they joined Simon, his relatives and his clerks in his house for worship. He arranged to have a portable Ark set up against the western wall. So when the Jews of Lancaster and several other nearby towns prayed they turned, as their fathers had done, toward Jerusalem. They remembered Zion in their prayers; but it is likely that every one of them silently thanked the God of Israel for bringing them to this goodly place.

On the Sabbath it was usually impossible to gather together the ten male Jews necessary for a service. But although surrounded by non-Jewish neighbors Joseph Simon scrupulously observed Saturday as a day of rest and refrained from transacting any business. He must have rejoiced in his later years when a synagogue was established in Philadelphia, where he might occasionally enjoy a Sabbath service.

When Joseph Simon died in 1804 his shrewd eyes had seen the thirteen colonies welded into a nation. The man of ninety-two was proud that he had done his share for freedom in helping supply the American troops with necessities during the Revolution. He surely must have rejoiced that his people would share the blessings of freedom which the soldiers of Washington had won. His work over, the patriarch was ready to find his deserved rest in the cemetery he had long ago purchased for the Jews of Lancaster.

.

AND NOW WE COME TO DELAWARE

Were there any Jews in the little colony of Delaware before the Revolution? We have no records of any ever settling there. But we do know that three Jews of New Amsterdam tried to gain permission to carry on their business along the Delaware River. This was in 1656. We have no way of knowing whether these hardy salesmen journeyed in the territory we now know as the colony of Delaware. If they made and left any maps of their travels they were lost long ago. The same uncertainty clouds the coming of the earliest Jews of New Hampshire and New Jersey.

A JEWISH DOCTOR IN MARYLAND

Maryland furnishes an unhappy contrast to the toleration we have just seen practised by the Friends. Lord Baltimore, the founder, was a Catholic. He hoped that his colony would prove a place of refuge for his co-religionists who suffered much discrimination in England. In his zeal for religious freedom, Baltimore welcomed so many Protestants that they in time outnumbered the Catholics. For a period they acted like the ungrateful camel in the fable and actually denied their benefactors certain civil rights.

It was promised, however, that no one professing to believe in Jesus Christ would be molested. This was the one thing no self-respecting Jew could promise. So in the early days of the colony with just one exception there is no record of our people settling in Maryland. There may have been a few transient traders now and then; if so, like their ancestors in the Spanish peninsula they were forced to live as secret Jews and we do not even know their names.

The one exception is a certain Jacob Lumbrozo who certainly made no effort to hide his Jewishness and is generally known as "the Jew doctor." We know nothing of his early life except that he was born in Portugal in 1600 and must have studied medicine, or at least have acted as a doctor's assistant in his middle age, before he came to Maryland.

He should have kept himself busy with his occasional medicinal practice and his trade with the Indians, but perhaps the religious persecutions he had seen in his native Portugal made him impatient with the teachings of Christianity. He was rash enough to argue with his neighbors on such delicate matters as the miracles and resurrection of Jesus, which he dared to deny. The doctor added other blasphemies for good measure, so he had only himself to blame when he was thrown into prison.

According to the harsh laws of that day he might have been punished by a long prison sentence or even death. Fortunately for the argumentative physician, just a few days after his arrest Oliver Cromwell, Lord Protector of England, died. Cromwell's son, who succeeded him, proclaimed a general amnesty which not only caused many vacancies in the London prisons but flung open the doors of Lumbrozo's jail house.

So instead of being forced to face a trial, Lumbrozo followed his fellow prisoners into a comparatively free world. It is likely he learned his lesson for we hear no more of his imprudent attacks on the religious beliefs of his neighbors. Instead of indulging in intemperate theological discussions, he seems to have devoted all his time to his medical practice and his business interests. The latter must have been very successful for he acquired quite a good deal of property before he died in 1666.

FIRST OF THE SOUTHERN COLONIES—VIRGINIA

The first Jew who is known to have lived in Virginia before the Revolution was Moses Nehemiah who was engaged in a lawsuit in that colony in 1658. Now and then we find Spanish or Portuguese names among the early settlers and are often tempted to assert that they belong to secret Jews, who had escaped from the Spanish peninsula to find safety in America. But as we have no record of any of these early settlers living as Jews, we cannot be at all sure of their religion.

But why did so few Jews seek to live in Virginia until around the time of the Revolution? A list giving a few legal restrictions should answer that question. Jews who would not acknowledge the divinity of Jesus could neither hold office nor vote in Virginia; along with other non-Christians, Negroes, Catholics and convicts they were disqualified as witnesses in a Virginia law court. Jews might not employ Christian servants; a Jew was taxed to support the state church, in this case the Church of England.

A few Jews drifted into the colony from time to time; because their small number made them inconspicuous there was no persecution. Still the majority, in spite of the many advantages Virginia might offer as a home, preferred to live elsewhere.

A GLANCE AT NORTH AND SOUTH CAROLINA

We can dismiss the matter of Jewish settlers in the early days of North Carolina with the statement: no record of any permanent Jewish settlement here before 1776. But there are several bits of information we have gleaned for you about the colony of South Carolina which we hope you will enjoy reading.

You may recall Luis de Torres, the secret Jew of 1492, when we read together one of the earliest records of South Carolina. It tells us that when the governor captured some Indian prisoners from Florida, he talked to them through a Jewish interpreter. The captives knew no other tongue but their own and the few phrases they had learned from their Spanish conquerors in the South; while the Jew remembered the language of his ancestors in far-off Spain.

To Charles Town, the colony's first settlement, came four Jews in 1697. Others rapidly followed; no doubt they were attracted by the promise of toleration as well as the excellent port which insured a flourishing trade with the West Indies.

By the fall Holy Days in 1749 there were enough Jews in Charles Town to organize and support a congregation, The House of God and Mansion of Peace. Several of the members served as rabbi and cantor.

The first hazan of Beth Elohim, to use the abbreviated Hebrew title, was the commission merchant, Isaac Da Costa of a celebrated Spanish-Portuguese family. How these refugee Jews wandered from country to country! Isaac Da Costa was reared in London; later he built up a successful business in both South Carolina and the neighboring colony of Georgia. But like many prominent merchants, Jewish and Christian, his conscience forced him to make heavy financial sacrifices in the economic struggle with England which preceded the Revolution.

A much greater sacrifice was made by another Jew from England, Francis Salvador, whose heroic story will be told in its proper place.

Remember that name which every son of South Carolina and every American Jew may repeat with pride.

GEORGIA, THE LAST OF THE THIRTEEN COLONIES

Everyone who has studied American history knows that the colony of Georgia was founded by an English philanthropist, General James Oglethorpe. It grieved him that Englishmen were often thrown into prison, to remain there under the most horrible conditions, because they were unable to pay their debts. Oglethorpe planned a colony where these unfortunate debtors might build a new life. He secured a large tract of land just below South Carolina, named it Georgia in honor of the

English king, and in 1732 brought over a shipful of prospective settlers.

Many others hoped to better their condition in the new colony. The promise of free, fertile land lured both Christians and Jews across the Atlantic to what seemed to be an earthly Paradise.

Shortly after the ship with Oglethorpe and his first settlers arrived, forty Sephardic Jews sailed into the harbor of the little settlement, which was one day to grow into the proud city of Savannah. They were not newly released debtors from the foul jails of London. Nearly all of the newcomers were men of property; it is more than likely that all of them would have succeeded had they chosen to remain in England.

For some reason they had grown restless in England; the bright face of adventure had lured them to seek greater opportunities in the new colony. But could they be sure of a welcome?

Oglethorpe was a generous, idealistic soul, but he was not

an impractical dreamer. He had already agreed with the trustees, who decided the political policies of Georgia, that it would be unwise to admit every immigrant who wished to settle there.

The Catholics were already excluded. But this exclusion was not based wholly on religious prejudice. The English Parliament had been in favor of establishing another colony below the Carolinas to act as a buffer against the Spaniards who still further south had claimed the vast wilderness of Florida for their king. Since these threatening neighbors were Catholics the trustees thought it necessary to pass such a law.

But Jews! The first Georgian settlers, who had just escaped from lives of poverty and degradation in London, feared the possible rivalry of these alien newcomers. Would these elegantly dressed strangers enrich themselves at the expense of those who still possessed nothing but the rags on their backs? These "first citizens" decided it was more than likely that such fine gentlemen would be too proud to work and expected to live on the sweat and toil of their neighbors.

General James Oglethorpe patiently listened to the angry accusations against the strangers. But he was a just man and was willing to listen also to the newly arrived Spanish Jews. He learned that some of them had brought enough capital to invest in business; better yet, their experience as London merchants would be helpful in developing Georgia's trade. Others promised that they, too, would add to the colony's welfare. They were experienced agriculturists and might prove at least

42

as useful as the willing but ignorant city dwellers, who were still pale from their confinement in a debtor's prison.

Such arguments convinced Oglethorpe. He was even more impressed by the courtliness and skill of one of the older gentlemen, Dr. Samuel Nunez. For many years he had practised as a physician in Lisbon; the Inquisition had suspected the Nunez family of backsliding and like so many Marranos they were forced to leave their native land. After many thrilling adventures Dr. Nunez arrived in London, from whence he sailed with his aged mother, hoping to make a home for her in Georgia.

Shortly after his arrival in Savannah Dr. Nunez found plenty of patients. For, according to one old record, something very like an epidemic broke out among the settlers. His ministrations were so successful that not a patient died. James Oglethorpe, the story ends, was so grateful that he rewarded the physician with a large tract of land.

In the same year a smaller group of Jews arrived. By this time the earlier Jewish immigrants had established themselves so solidly that few voices were raised in protest against the newcomers. None of the Christian settlers felt envious of them for they were poor German Jews sent over the sea by their rich co-religionists of London. Like the English debtors the Jews of this second migration were so anxious to earn a decent living for themselves and their families that they worked hard from the moment of their arrival. It was not hard for their Gentile neighbors to tolerate and soon to respect them for their honesty and industry.

More than once in this history we have been obliged to repeat some story of bigotry or hatred. So it is good to be able to tell a little tale recorded by one of the earliest Jewish settlers in the Georgia colony.

Shortly after the second shipload of Jews sailed into the Savannah harbor, a group of German Protestants arrived from Salzburg. Oglethorpe received them kindly but the simple peasants seemed bewildered and afraid among so many strangers. And no one, they were sure, could speak to them or understand their language.

But a few German Jews quickly showed them how mistaken they were. A kindly old couple, chattering eagerly in the language of their native land, took several of the newcomers to their hut and set hot potato soup before them. The German Protestants almost wept with joy. Who could have expected to taste such soup, real German potato soup, in the backwoods of America, they asked each other over their steaming bowls.

The next morning the German Jew sighed heavily as he left his hut to begin his day's ploughing. He was no longer young; the sun was hot; for a moment he wished he were back in London. But could he still be in bed and dreaming? For his fields were ploughed and ready for their first sowing. Yes, you've guessed it. The German peasants had repaid their Jewish neighbor for his potato soup. A very trivial story, but we think it deserves a place in our chronicle.

TO SUM UP THE STORY OF EARLY JEWISH SETTLEMENT IN AMERICA:

In our travels with the first Jews who came to settle in the American colonies we have seen how their history repeats itself again and again. There was never a real migration. Usually we discover a small group of the wandering people who seek a refuge, or perhaps one family, or sometimes even a single, lonely adventurer. We see the newcomers along with their pioneer neighbors, building their rude homes, establishing themselves on the land or in trade. In time they must purchase a bit of land for a cemetery; if it is possible to gather together ten adult males for religious worship, there is a temporary and in a few cases a permanent synagogue.

Some colonies granted these Jews a grudging welcome; others raised no opposing barriers to their entrance, but denied them certain civil rights. Everywhere the Jews were a group outside the dominant church. For them there could be no true equality until the principle of the separation of church and state came into being with the newly created United States of America.

There were fewer than three thousand Jews scattered through the thirteen colonies, which were shortly to begin their desperate struggle against the tyranny of King George III. Because so many of these Jews were merchants they played a prominent part in the ever-mounting protest movements directed against England's unjust trade regulations.

Pioneer traders like Bernard and Michael Gratz were among the Philadelphia merchants who pledged themselves as early as 1765 not to import goods from England. There were a number of other Jewish business men who signed the 1765 agreement which they hoped would bring about the repeal of the hateful Stamp Act. But this group did not suffer so severely from its defiance of the Mother Country as the Jewish merchants of Newport, headed by Aaron Lopez.

These men depended almost entirely on England for their manufactured goods. Defying England meant hampering their business and in the end financial ruin; but they did not falter. The Jewish merchants of Newport knew the meaning of tyranny and bondage; now that they dwelt in a land of freedom, they were willing to pledge their fortunes to secure justice.

Aaron Lopez, the most successful of Newport merchants, had the most to lose. When he could no longer import English goods to be used for barter with foreign countries, his trade declined rapidly. When the war broke out his gallant ships could not withstand the British navy. When the British captured Newport, Aaron Lopez, a marked man because of his loyalty to the American cause, was obliged to seek safety in Leicester, Massachusetts. Other Jews from the once thriving little seaport town followed him. When the Revolution ended, many of them returned to Newport. But Aaron Lopez was not among them. He died as he journeyed along the road to the spot where he had spent so many happy years. His mourning friends brought the patriot's body back to rest in the Jewish cemetery at Newport.

JEWISH IDEALS WHICH INFLUENCED THE BUILDERS OF OUR COUNTRY

We are fast approaching the page in our story which tells how a group of colonial gentlemen on a very hot July day gathered in Philadelphia. The signers of the Declaration of Independence had few if any acquaintances among the Jews scattered through the colonies from Rhode Island to Georgia. Thomas Jefferson of Virginia, John Hancock of Massachusetts, Caesar Rodney who had ridden like mad that little Delaware might be represented, probably never met a single Jew until they visited New York or Philadelphia. But the still living idealism of the ancient Hebrews filled the hearts of these fathers of American liberty.

The Puritans had brought with them across the sea the deepest reverence for the Old Testament. They did more than reverence the Book which through daily reading became a part of their lives. They loved to give their children Scriptural names, often so cumbersome when translated that we wonder how old the youngsters were before they could pronounce them properly. Often their towns bore the names of Hebrew cities. Many of the early laws of Massachusetts were drawn from the Bible's legal codes; the earliest celebrations of Thanksgiving, although they may have been suggested by the English Harvest Home festivals, closely resembled our old, old feast of Succoth.

We have seen the importance which in the early days Harvard College gave to Hebrew. The influence of the Old Testament was not confined to ministers and scholars. Not only the Puritans but the other colonists knew their Bible. In a day when only the rich or the cultured collected books, the Bible was often the family's entire library. A man who could read would turn to it for his poetry, his stories, even his political ideas.

Just an example or two! As the clouds of war darkened the horizon of America, preachers compared the tyranny of the British king to the cruel rule of Pharaoh in Egypt, confident that their listeners would understand. In 1776 Benjamin Franklin, John Adams and Thomas Jefferson designed what they hoped would be the seal for the newly born United States. They suggested that it show the escape of the Israelites from Egyptian bondage. While a Quaker selected from the Book of Leviticus the words for the inscription of a bell which hung in a Philadelphia tower.

The words were: "Proclaim liberty throughout the land, unto all the inhabitants thereof." The bell was the Liberty Bell which gave a waiting world the message that the Declaration of Independence had been adopted.

AN EARLY AMERICAN MARTYR

We have all heard of Crispus, the Negro whose life blood stained the snows on Boston Common when the British troops fired and brought low "the first martyr of the Revolution." But few know the story of our Jewish martyr to American liberty, Francis Salvador, who in August of the year 1776 sacrificed his life for his country's freedom.

Francis Salvador was the nephew of Joseph Salvador, a prominent and immensely wealthy London Jew, who about twenty years before the Revolution had purchased thousands of acres of land in South Carolina. Young Salvador, a true pioneer, came to the colony in 1773; although he had had no experience as a planter, he was from the first successful in raising indigo. Before long he had added land of his own to his uncle's vast possessions and became the owner of 7,000 acres and many slaves.

The young planter could not forget certain injustices his people still suffered in England. A number of wealthy Jews, including the Salvadors, had aided the British government by securing sorely needed loans. If they expected the government to show its gratitude by allowing Jews to share the civil rights of English citizens they were sorely disappointed. Joseph Salvador was outraged when Jews whom he had helped to emigrate to South Carolina returned to England with stories of having become naturalized citizens. This was a boon no English Jew could obtain at that time. No wonder that twenty-six-year-old Francis Salvador, riding about his flourishing plantation, or reading in his library at night, felt so bitter toward England.

"It is not only England's injustice and ingratitude to my own people," he told his new Christian friends. "What of the injustice and ingratitude the king and his Parliament now practise against us in this new world we are trying to build for ourselves and our children?"

The Tories turned against Francis Salvador as a trouble-maker and rebel, but many of his neighbors shared his ideas. His Christian friends must have admired and trusted him; for two years after he came to the colony, we find him serving as a member of the Second Provincial Congress of South Carolina. When in 1776 South Carolina joined her sister colonies in the fight for independence, this body became the General Assembly. Still a member, Francis Salvador won the distinction of being the first Jew to serve in an American legislative body. For the aggressive planter was so generally respected

Francis Salvador in the General Assembly

that his neighbors did not trouble themselves over the old Carolina law that only Christians might hold office.

Francis Salvador had once loved the coming of summer to the Carolinas with the long days bright with sunshine and the fields teeming with increase. But in the year 1776 June brought war, undeclared as yet, but with all of a war's terror and desolation. The British launched a two-fold attack on Carolina. In

51

the last week of June the army and navy attacked Charles Town. While a little later in the back country the Indians, urged on by the Tories, spread havoc among the ill-protected colonists.

Days desperate with anxiety followed. A youth named Smith staggered across the lawn before Salvador's mansion. He thrust forth his maimed hand and mumbled that two of the fingers had been shot off as he battled with the attacking Indians. Between his sobs he described the deaths of his parents, his brother and his sister.

Salvador ordered a slave to care for the exhausted youth. He sprang to the saddle and urged his horse into a merciless gallop. He knew he must not waste a minute in reporting to Major Andrew Williamson who lived almost thirty miles away.

The two men, both members of the state militia, now worked side by side to raise enough men to repel further frontier attacks. It was not easy to secure volunteers. Those with Tory sympathies secretly rejoiced and hoped that before long South Carolina's rebels against the king would either be massacred or frightened into submission. Others believed in the Revolution but seemed willing to endanger the cause by delays; they declared they were ready to fight but not in a regiment commanded by a mere major. Many poor men with no slaves to work their land insisted they could not risk their lives in battle until their dependent families had been promised security.

Yet the original company of forty patriots doubled over

night. As the danger increased the regiment grew; Salvador soon reported that it had increased to five hundred. This number was augmented by two companies which added over four hundred men.

Francis Salvador rode beside his friend, Major Williamson, in the heavy pre-dawn darkness of an August morning. What were his thoughts as his horse's hooves dashed the dew from the tangling grasses of the frontier? How good it would be when the savages were driven back and a planter might in all honor spend his days riding across his own peaceful fields. Or: How much it would have meant to have been in Philadelphia last month to represent South Carolina and to add his name to the proud roll of signers of Mr. Jefferson's Declaration of Independence. Or, perhaps: Who could have dreamed that I, a London Jew, would be called upon to face the murderous redskins of the frontier?

We cannot know his thoughts, but there is a record of his dying words. Shortly after the Indians leaped from their ambush, young Francis Salvador fell from his horse. Thrice wounded, and bleeding from an enemy's scalping knife, Salvador lingered in pain while the battle raged about him.

Almost an hour later his dim eyes recognized the sorrowful face of Major Williamson who bent over him. Francis Salvador gathered the little strength that was in him for only one question.

"The battle?" he asked faintly.

"We have defeated the Indians," answered Williamson.

The dying soldier grasped his friend's hand. In the midst of his agony his smile was so triumphant that the major knew he was happy in his death.

So Francis Salvador died, the first of those who have played a part in Jewish adventures in America to die for this republic. At least in Charleston (its official name since 1783) he will never be forgotten for every school child in that lovely city can direct the visitor to a memorial in City Hall Park. It bears this tribute to the Jew who gave his all for freedom:

> Born an aristocrat, he became a democrat,
> An Englishman, he cast his lot with America;
> True to his ancient faith, he gave his life
> For new hopes of human liberty and understanding.

AMERICAN PATRIOTS AND TORIES IN THE FRANKS FAMILY

Another Jew, also young, devoted and brave, was Isaac Franks. More fortunate in his war experiences than Salvador, he also traced his descent from a famous Jewish family, in this case originating in Germany. Still under twenty, Isaac lived in New York during the first thrilling days of the war. We like to think he joined the excited mob at Bowling Green which tore down the leaden statue of George III that it might be melted into patriotic bullets. It is also likely that, dressed in the new uniform he had purchased himself even before he joined the army, the youth stood among his fellow-soldiers to hear an officer of George Washington's staff read the Declaration of Independence.

While serving with this company of New York volunteers, he took part in the Battle of Long Island. After General Washington's retreat, Franks was imprisoned by the victorious British who captured New York City. He managed to escape and to make his perilous way across the Hudson in a small boat. Later he served both in the infantry and quartermaster branches of the American army and received numerous promotions.

He was proud to receive the rank of Lieutenant Colonel from the Pennsylvania militia in which he had served as an officer after the war. But perhaps Franks was even prouder of the fact that his home had once sheltered his beloved Commander in Chief. For when yellow fever raged in Philadelphia, at that time the new nation's capital, President Washington to escape the epidemic lived in the mansion Isaac Franks had built for himself in the suburb of Germantown.

Another member of the Franks family to win renown as a soldier was David Salisbury Franks, who had settled in Canada. He continued to conduct his business in Montreal during the first months of the war. Although his neighbors were nearly all fiercely loyal to the British crown, this Jewish merchant did all in his power to aid the thirteen colonies in their desperate need. In 1775 General Montgomery led his victorious troops into Montreal, where Franks secured supplies to feed the American army and even lent his own money to pay Montgomery's men their wages. This did not endear the Jewish merchant to his Tory neighbors; when the Americans were forced to withdraw from Canada, David S. Franks prudently followed them back to the United States.

Serving as a volunteer, he rose rapidly in the ranks; before long we find Major David Salisbury Franks serving as aide to General Benedict Arnold. Later when Benedict Arnold turned traitor, this position of trust and responsibility brought suspicion and near disgrace to Franks. But he demanded a court martial in which he was able to prove his innocence. He not only retained his rank, but was even trusted with several important diplomatic missions. When he retired from the army he held the rank of Lieutenant-Colonel.

The records of these two men did much to save the reputation of the Franks family, since all loyal Americans came to despise one of its ablest members. This was David Franks, an indifferent Jew and a Tory.

One of his daughters, Rebecca, seems to have been as friendly as her father to the invaders of her country. While Washington's sorely tried little army starved in the bleakness of Valley Forge, in nearby Philadelphia Miss Franks welcomed the victorious red-coated officers and listened complacently while they praised her beauty and laughed at her sharp and nimble wit. Her cleverly phrased letters are filled with descriptions of the latest fashion, of her triumphs as the belle of the gay balls given by the British staff and their Tory supporters.

Perhaps her greatest moment came when she was chosen as one of the two Queens of Beauty at a twelve-hour-long fete, the Meschianza. Gorgeously dressed, with jewels sparkling on her proud little head, she made her courtesy to the British general, Sir William Howe, and flirted with her gifted admirer, Major John Andre.

But young Andre for all his gallantry and charm was destined to die as a spy on the gallows. And a month after the Meschianza with its dancing and feasting and fireworks, the British marched out of Philadelphia, to meet at Monmouth a crushing defeat from the despised Americans.

David Franks and his light-minded daughter were banished from Philadelphia when the colonials again occupied that city. Fortunately for Rebecca, who always loved what she considered the "best society," they were sent to New York City, which was still held by the British. Here the young woman occupied her time with dancing and observing the latest fashions and flirting with her many English admirers. She finally chose one to be her husband, Lieutenant Colonel Henry Johnson, who after the war took her to England.

Her father followed her but later returned to end his years in the United States. The war had cost him a considerable proportion of his once impressive fortune as well as the friendship and respect of the majority of his former friends. We have never run across any statement which suggests that in the loneliness of old age he regretted the part he had played in his country's struggle for independence.

But a story has come down to us of Rebecca Franks which suggests something of the despair and shame of her countryman, Benedict Arnold. It is said that in his English exile he requested to be buried in his American uniform, adding in explanation: "I have never been happy since I put it aside." Rebecca Franks in her carefree youth had shown no loyalty either as American or Jew; in her exiled old age she spoke admiringly of the American fighters in the War of 1812. "Would to God I too had been a patriot," sighed Rebecca.

OF BENJAMIN NONES AND THE PINTO BROTHERS

Benjamin Nones, born in France, arrived in Philadelphia during the trying days of 1777. He entered the badly organized, ill-equipped colonial army as a private, but rose to the rank of major and became one of the officers of General Washington's staff. At the end of the eight-year-long war he received a citation for bravery in the field.

By this time he considered America as his true home. He settled in Philadelphia, married and raised his family. He was active in Jewish affairs; for many years he served Congregation Mikveh Israel as its president. Always interested in politics, he decided to run for office. During the campaign he answered with humorous defiance some of the charges that his political opponents had brought against him.

"I am accused," he stated, "of being a Jew, of being a Republican, and of being poor—three things which make me more worthy of being elected."

You may remember the Pinto family of Connecticut which the Rev. Ezra Stiles criticized for its lack of religious devotion. But its sons were loyal Americans, who fought bravely and well in the colonial army; one of them, Solomon, was an officer in the regiment of his native state. Two of the Pinto brothers felt especially grateful to the country which had given their people refuge. For at a time when it was always difficult and usually impossible for a Jew to enter a European university, these young men were permitted to graduate from Yale.

THE "JEWS' COMPANY" OF CHARLESTON AND A HERO FROM GEORGIA

The largest group of Jewish soldiers from any one colony came from South Carolina. In fact, a company in Charleston was often referred to as the "Jews' company" because of the many Jews enrolled. There were twenty-six Jews among these defenders of Charleston, a large number when one considers the proportion of Jewish able-bodied men to the rest of the city's male population. After the British capture of the city, many of these defenders suffered imprisonment or banishment.

Among Southern fighters for the Revolution we always find the name of Mordecai Sheftall of Georgia, who held an important post until he had the misfortune to be captured by the British. A prison ship carried him to the West Indies, where he suffered many privations and hardships. His health was broken by his sufferings before he was exchanged for certain British prisoners and restored to his home.

ONE WORD MORE ABOUT JEWISH SOLDIERS IN THE REVOLUTION

You may wonder why so few Jews served as soldiers during the Revolutionary War. But don't forget how few Jews acceptable to the army could be found in all the thirteen colonies! At that time the entire Jewish population was considerably less than three thousand souls; twenty-five hundred seems a likelier figure. That meant that only a few hundred Jews were of military age. Of course, because of faulty records we cannot be sure just how many served. But we have the names of about fifty Jews who enlisted in the continental armies, including the group in the Charleston militia.

THOSE WHO FOUGHT IN THEIR OWN WAY

We have said little, since little is known, of the men in the ranks who risked their lives for liberty. In the scattered Jewish communities we find many citizens who might also be termed "privates." These patriots behind the lines risked much, for if the Revolution had failed the leaders would have been punished as rebels. Planters like Francis Salvador and merchants like Aaron Lopez knew that the defeat of the colonials meant that their wealth would be confiscated. Yet there were very few Jewish Tories like David Franks; the majority of Jews did not shrink from the many sacrifices the war imposed on the civilian population.

61

Again and again the war radically changed the lives of many men and women; often they were forced to make decisions that meant great personal sacrifices. Rabbi Gershom Mendes Seixas was not a merchant prince; he had no fortune to lose; in fact the salary he received from his New York congregation was quite small even for those days of modest living and low incomes. But when he was forced to make his great decision he did not falter.

Gershom Mendes Seixas is usually called "rabbi," meaning in this case the leader of a congregation. Actually he was cantor of Shearith Israel. He was born in New York, which makes him the first Jewish religious leader to be born on this side of the Atlantic. His father was Sephardic, his mother of Ashkenazic ancestry. Their marriage helps us realize how at that period the two groups mingled socially and even "intermarried." We realize, too, how quickly the descendants of the earlier Jewish immigrants to New York were being absorbed into the society about them; for young Seixas does not seem to have been able to read or speak either Spanish or Portuguese.

Nor does he appear, from all we have learned about him, to have had much knowledge of Hebrew; certainly not enough to qualify him as a rabbi. Of course, in this period there were no seminaries in America for the training of rabbis. The very few Jewish scholars who came to this country were scattered through the country. In New York City a boy eager for a Jewish education would have to be satisfied with what he could learn in an elementary Hebrew school. So the youth supplemented what he was taught there by self-instruction and reading. Since it seemed impossible to lure ordained rabbis from abroad, Congregation Shearith Israel decided that Gershom Mendes Seixas had sufficient Jewish knowledge to be their leader. Except for one tragic interlude he served as their "rabbi" for forty-eight years.

Rabbi Seixas left New York in 1776. He had shuddered to hear of the advance of the victorious British forces; how General Washington, after masking a battery of guns behind the trees which surrounded the Jewish cemetery, had been forced to retreat. As an American patriot, the rabbi felt he could not live and work in a community which had lost its liberty. It was not easy for him to leave his birthplace and the friends who remained behind; he could not be sure when and where he would be able to serve another congregation. And, like every conspicuous rebel who dared defy the British king, Seixas faced imprisonment or even a traitor's death if his countrymen were defeated.

Many of the congregation agreed with their rabbi and prepared to follow him into self-imposed exile. It was a hurried flight and few were fortunate enough to have time to gather many valuable possessions. But all insisted that the Scroll of the Law must not remain behind. Rabbi Seixas went to the Ark in his little synagogue and lifted out the Torah, Israel's greatest treasure through the wandering years. Then, wanderers as their fathers had been before them, a number of the members of Shearith Israel joined their leader in his flight to Connecticut.

Here they remained for several years. Gradually family after family moved to Philadelphia to join the growing Jewish community in that city. In three years these war refugees urged their former rabbi to join them. Arriving in Philadelphia, Rabbi Seixas reorganized the services of Mikveh Israel Congregation and later took part in dedicating its new synagogue.

When the war was over and the New York congregation wrote to Rabbi Seixas and urged him to return, the Jews of Philadelphia tried to persuade him to remain with them. At least, they insisted, until after Passover, which was then less than a month away. They added, as a final argument, that by spring it would be easier to travel the winter-weathered roads between the two cities. But a spokesman for the New York congregation insisted that as long as the Philadelphians were going to lose their rabbi, it might be just as well to release him at once. But he was polite enough to wish everyone who belonged to Mikveh Israel all the joys of the Passover season!

So Rabbi Gershom Mendes Seixas returned to New York

to live many more useful years in the city of his birth. He was not the man to expect a reward for doing what he considered his duty, but he must have been pleased at one of the many honors he received because it also brought honor to his fellow Jews. For while it was still undreamed of for a Jew to teach in a college or serve on its board of directors, Rabbi Seixas was asked to act as one of the trustees of Columbia.

The rabbi seems to have been very happy in his family life. One of his letters gives a delightful picture of a Purim party. After a supper of "tea, sweet loaves and ginger bread," he kept the willing children around his chair until long past their usual bedtime and told them of the thrilling days when the British ships sailed into New York harbor.

He lived to be a very old man, beloved and honored not only by his own congregation but by all his Gentile neighbors. Jew and Christian grieved together on the day when the altar in the Mill Street synagogue was draped in black to symbolize that the war-time rabbi's labors were over.

THE PATRIOTIC BROKER OF THE REVOLUTION

Enough pleasant nonsense has been written about Haym Salomon to fill a book several times the size of this volume. He is really the Jewish folk hero of the Revolutionary War. And everybody knows how easy it is to make up—and believe!

—legends about a folk hero. In this case the proven facts are so exciting that we will stick to the truth—if we can.

We do not know the exact date when Haym Salomon arrived in New York, but it was either in the year 1775 or 1776. He had wandered in many lands after leaving his native Poland in his youth; in his travels he had gathered an amazing knowledge of many languages, among them German, French, Russian and English. Salomon had visited the leading commercial centers in Europe and studied the methods of the leading bankers and brokers. This training with his own genius for finance seemed sure to bring him success in the business circles of New York City.

But the confusion and uncertainty of war made it impossible for Haym Salomon to establish himself immediately as a broker. In the summer of 1776 we find him acting as sutler to the colonial troops at Lake George in upper New York State. Too ambitious to remain a peddler, he returned to the big city.

Here his adventures, which have been much embroidered through the years, began. There is no real proof that he joined the Liberty Boys, a secret group which aided the American cause by frequent acts of sabotage such as setting the New York wharves on fire to endanger the British fleet. But we do know that the enemy believed the energetic Polish Jew menaced their interests; to quote from one of Salomon's own letters, the British locked him up "as a spy."

Salomon, according to his own account, spent his time in prison serving the American cause. Because of his knowledge of languages he was able to make himself useful as interpreter to the prisoners who knew no English. He helped a number of them to escape possibly because he was able to talk to the Hessian guards in their native German. We can easily believe that these unfortunate mercenaries, sold by their masters to serve under the English flag, were homesick and ready to desert. And that more than once Haym Salomon helped them to decide by repeating the colonial government's offer of free land to any German soldiers who came over to the American side.

We are not sure whether Mr. Salomon was released from prison or managed to escape through his friendship with the Hessians. But there is plenty of evidence that the British authorities began to learn of his activities; he fled to Philadelphia, which was in American hands.

Here Mr. Salomon's real services to the American cause really began. The history books tell us of Robert Morris' struggle to secure funds that the impoverished colonies might continue the war. But for many years the historians were strangely silent concerning the Jewish broker whose name the Superintendent of Finance mentioned over a hundred times in his diary. For as time went on Salomon became Morris's right-hand man in negotiating loans from foreign powers.

Besides helping to establish foreign credit for the struggling, new-born nation, Haym Salomon aided many of the leaders of the Revolution. Few delegates to the Continental Congress were wealthy; the states they represented promised to pay necessary expenses, but could not afford to do so, or were shockingly tardy in their payments. A young man, James Madison, later to become President of these United States, gave some idea of Salomon's generosity to himself and others, when he stated:

"I have been a pensioner for some time on the favor of Haym Salomon. The kindness of our friend is a fund that will preserve me from extremities, but I never resort to it without great mortification, as he obstinately rejects all recompense. To necessitous delegates he always spares them supplies."

During the Philadelphia years Salomon identified himself closely with the Jewish community of that city. We are told he sent to Europe for a Torah for the growing congregation. As one of the trustees he protested to the State of Pennsylvania against a "religious test" which would bar Jews from public office. When the time arrived to build a synagogue in the Quaker City, the ever generous broker donated over a third of the entire sum collected.

Mr. Salomon seems to have been shocked at the type of Judaism he found in the New World and in one of his letters he warns a pious uncle to stay in Europe where he will be happier in his religion. But as Haym Salomon knew that his uncle expected his rich nephew to care for him if he came to America, the letter may have been written to induce him to stay at home!

The times, both during the war and the years which followed, were filled with uncertainties for even shrewd business men. Fortunes were quickly acquired and as quickly lost. Haym Salomon is said to have made and lost a considerable fortune during his early years in New York. He came to Philadelphia almost penniless and again acquired considerable wealth. But now that the war was ended, the recently established United States suffered from a terrible depression. Many merchants who owed Salomon money were unable to pay their debts, and the patriotic broker had signed many bills and drafts which the government now found impossible to honor.

We do not believe he mourned his financial ruin. He must have worried, of course, when he became very ill and began to wonder who would take care of his young wife and four little children. But there is not a single record of his regret over his sacrifice. If the government he had served so long and so faithfully was too poor to repay him, he must have felt fully recompensed to have had a share in bringing victory to the land which had proved a haven to his people.

His death was scarcely noticed in the excitement and confusion of building a new nation. For years Haym Salomon's brilliance, his devotion to his faith and to his country were forgotten. But little by little historians blew the gathered dust from their records. The Jews of America read the story of the broker of the Revolution and awarded him their tardy

ROBERT MORRIS · GEORGE WASHINGTON · HAYM SALOMON

praise, especially the Polish Jews of the United States who proudly claimed this early immigrant as their own. They collected money for a statue which today stands in one of Chicago's largest parks. Of heroic size, it shows George Washington standing between two of his supporters, Robert Morris and Haym Salomon. It is a fitting memorial to the devoted and fearless little broker of the Revolution.

How would you like to read the letter our first President wrote to the Jews of Newport?

When General George Washington was elected President of the United States, there were six congregations scattered through our country. Each sent him good wishes and a pledge of loyalty to the new government. There were carefully and elegantly phrased letters from Savannah and Charleston in the South and Newport, Rhode Island. The older congregations of New York and Philadelphia joined the very recent group in Richmond, Virginia, in a congratulatory letter.

President Washington replied to these messages with his well-known politeness. The heavy eloquence of the period could not hide his sincerity; he seems to have been really touched by the friendliness of the Jews who had supported him so loyally during the war. But before we turn to perhaps the most famous of these replies, let us read just one sentence from the message of the Newport congregation:

"Deprived as we have hitherto been of the invaluable rights of free citizens we now, (with a deep sense of gratitude to the Almighty Disposer of all events) behold a Government (erected by the Majesty of the People) a Government which to bigotry gives no sanction, to persecution no assistance—but generously affording to all liberty of conscience, and immunities of citizenship—deeming every one, of whatever nation, tongue, or language equal parts of the great governmental machine."

In the opening lines of his reply, the president refers graciously to the reception he received in Newport on his visit there "from all classes of citizens." As Jews we are especially interested in this visit. The State House had been burned. The story goes that because no other building in Newport was large enough to seat the members of the legislature Washington expected to address, several Jewish citizens offered the use of the synagogue. To this day the caretaker of the beautiful white building proudly shows every visitor the chair where President Washington sat and sometimes brings out a yellowed newspaper clipping describing his visit.

The President's answer stresses the principle idea of his Jewish wellwishers which we have quoted above. He writes:

"The Citizens of the United States of America have a right to applaud themselves for having given to mankind examples of a large and liberal policy, a policy worthy of imitation.

"All possess alike liberty of conscience and immunities of citizenship. It is now no more that toleration is spoken of, as if it was by the indulgence of one class of people, that another enjoyed the exercise of their inherent natural rights. For happily the government of the United States, which give to bigotry no sanction, to persecution no assistance, requires only that they who live under its protection should demean themselves as good citizens, in giving it on all occasions their

72

effectual support.

"May the children of the stock of Abraham, who dwell in this land, continue to merit and enjoy the good will of the other inhabitants, while every one shall sit in safety under his own vine and fig-tree, and there shall be none to make him afraid. . . .

G. Washington."

part two

WE GROW
WITH AMERICA

Look over my shoulder and read with me an item in a yellowed newspaper preserved from the year 1788. It tells of a city-wide celebration in Philadelphia in honor of the ratification of the newly adopted Constitution of the United States. We Jews had a part in it; one of the marchers in the parade was Raphael Jacob Cohen, the minister of Mikveh Israel congregation.

"The Clergy," runs the newspaper story before us, "formed a very agreeable part of the procession. They manifested by their attendance, their sense of the connection between religion and good government. They amounted to seventeen in number. Four and five of them marched arm in arm with each other to exemplify the Union. . . . The Rabbi of the Jews, locked in the arms of two ministers of the gospel, was a most delightful sight. There could not have been a more happy emblem contrived, of that section of the new Constitution, which opens all its powers and offices alike, not only to every sect of Christian, but to worthy men of *every* religion."

A certain portly, bespectacled fellow-townsman of the journalist who penned these lines must have heartily agreed. We can see the aged Benjamin Franklin adjusting his bifocals to reread the account which so well reflected the spirit of the new Constitution. Franklin had helped to bring the Constitution into being. The statesman and philosopher, although not a member of any church, was a friend "to worthy men of *every* religion." Before we lay the pile of old newspapers aside, let me show you the record of Benjamin Franklin's contribution to the building fund of the local synagogue.

No wonder that the Constitution with its Bill of Rights was hailed not only by the Jews of the United States but by their less fortunate brethren in distant lands. Even such enlightened countries as Holland and England still made distinctions between their Christian citizens and the Jews. Certain restrictions might be lifted and certain freedoms granted our people, but only through special acts passed by the government.

But the Constitution did not regard the Jewish citizens of this country as a separate body which required separate laws. For the first time since the Romans conquered Palestine, the Jewish people could rejoice that they lived in a land with no one privileged church, a land which as a constitutional right granted them freedom to practice their own religion. And, best of all, they received this privilege not as Jews but as citizens of a free Republic.

So the Jews of Philadelphia in 1788 did well to rejoice that they were at last recognized as citizens all over the United States.

But freedom is a plant of slow growth even if it is carefully tended by such lovers of liberty as Thomas Jefferson and James Madison. As early as 1776 Virginia had adopted its own

Bill of Rights which stated: "That all men are by nature equally free and independent, and have certain inherent rights . . . the enjoyment of life and liberty, with the means of acquiring and possessing property, and pursuing and obtaining happiness and safety." The words have a familiar ring! A month later one of Virginia's ablest sons, the lanky, red-headed Thomas Jefferson, remembered them when he drafted the Declaration of Independence.

But even in the progressive state of Virginia, it was not until 1786 that Jefferson's Bill for Establishing Religious Freedom became a law. Since Jefferson at that time was acting as Ambassador to France, he depended on his young neighbor and protege, James Madison, to fight for its enactment. Thomas Jefferson wished recorded on his tombstone as one of the greatest achievements of his life the fact that he had drawn up this bill to ensure religious freedom to every citizen in his native state.

It had taken six years of hard fighting to pass this bill. At that time there were fewer than twenty-five Jewish families living in the entire state of Virginia; but this legislation was of the greatest importance to our people, and not to Jews

79

alone. For it greatly influenced the doctrine of the separation of Church and State, which appeared in the Federal Constitution, a doctrine which was to prove of the greatest value to the new nation.

We have told the story of the slow growth of religious freedom in Virginia because it is typical of the struggle which went on all over the country, even after the Constitution was ratified. Not even a war fought for liberty and finally won could bring complete justice and freedom in a single month or year. But very aged Jews who remembered the stories their fathers had told of early trials in the colonies realized how much had been accomplished. The principle of religious liberty, they said, had been won. It would take some time to enforce it in every detail. They turned hopeful faces to the future.

Religious Ornaments by Myer Myers, Silversmith

We have seen how many of the Jews who came to the colonies engaged in trade, from the merchant princes of Newport and Philadelphia down to the solitary peddlers who followed the Indian trails through the wilderness. And some, you remember, opened shops like Joseph Simon of Lancaster, or Judah Monis whose students seem to have preferred his pipes to his Hebrew grammar.

There were practically no Jewish doctors in the period before and just after the Revolution, and no Jewish lawyers. Our only Jewish professional men were our cantors and Hebrew teachers in a few of the larger communities.

In the South there were a few plantation owners like Francis Salvador. But the Jew who for centuries had been forbidden to own land was not yet ready to engage in farming. For one reason, until our own time, life on a farm meant he would be cut off from his own people; he could not join other Jews in religious and cultural activities; it was impossible to give his children a Jewish education. So whenever he could the Jew settled in a city where there was already a Jewish community.

It is very likely you have heard all this before; but you may not know how many Jews in early America worked with their hands. We have records of Jews who made soap and candles and snuff; of others who manufactured saddles and watches.

We know of at least three who were masters of the crafts they practised. Isaiah Isaacs who lived in Richmond was a distinguished silversmith. There were also the two Myers brothers. They were both merchants and craftsmen. Asher worked in brass while Myer was a silversmith. The work of the latter is highly prized even today and is exhibited in many art museums. A number of churches and synagogues still use the treasured ceremonial objects he made for them. For Congregation Shearith Israel of which he was president he created the silver bells which ornament its Torah scrolls.

JEWISH LIFE AFTER THE REVOLUTION

Now there was no need for Jewish newcomers to ask permission of the government to erect a synagogue. Of course, in isolated sections with just a handful of Jews it was still difficult to gather the required number for public worship. Sometimes, too, it was very hard to collect funds; often, as in the case of the Newport congregation, it was necessary to appeal to Jews of other communities to help build a new synagogue.

We remember how when the first Jews came to New Amsterdam the Dutch rulers would not permit them to establish a place for public worship. The little congregation which was forced to worship in private homes called itself Shearith Israel. The name was painfully appropriate; for these war refugees surely felt that they were the "remnant of Israel." When they were forced to flee from Recife, instead of returning to Holland with the hundreds and hundreds of other Spanish and Portuguese Jews, the twenty-three elected ones had somehow drifted to the colony on the bank of the Hudson.

It is not known exactly when the English government, which deposed the Dutch, gave the Jews of Shearith Israel permission to build their own house of worship. But by 1729 they erected a humble building which looked for all the world like a small hut. It was located on Mill Street; but even if you live in New York City and are interested in historical sites, do not try to find it. One nearby building seems to have served as a school house; two others sheltered the rabbi and the caretaker.

Gradually the Jewish congregation moved to what was then considered "uptown." In 1833 Shearith Israel congregation erected a new and larger building on Crosby Street. Almost thirty years later the group again moved "uptown"—this time to 19th Street.

By this time Shearith Israel was no longer the only synagogue in New York City. As it had been established by the descendants of Spanish and Portuguese Jews its ritual had been Sephardic. Later so many Ashkenazim came to the city and joined the congregation that they actually outnumbered the Sephardic worshippers. They accepted the ritual of the

GROWTH OF SYNAGOGUES IN THE UNITED STATES

1790

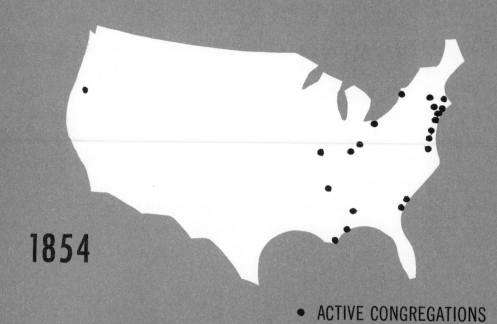

1854

• ACTIVE CONGREGATIONS

former as well as their unfamiliar pronunciation of the Hebrew prayers.

It was not until 1825 that the Jews who came from Central Europe formed the second synagogue in New York City. At first there was an understandable rivalry between the two congregations. But before very long Shearith Israel and Bnai Jeshurun (sons of Israel) began to exchange courtesies. A leading member of the new group asked permission to have his son make his bar mitzvah at the older synagogue. We can understand the reason for the father's request and why the favor was granted by the trustees of Shearith Israel. For the boy was a grandson of Gershom Mendes Seixas, who had served that congregation for so many years. It is pleasant to read that these same trustees attended the consecration services of Bnai Jeshurun and lent four scrolls to be used during the ceremony.

Now every few years a group made up largely of newcomers established another synagogue. It would take too long even to list the many congregations which began before the Civil War; in many cases they are still functioning. Many of them were formed by Jews who had come from the same country. The early membership of Shearith Israel had been made up of the dwindling Sephardim and English, German and Polish Jews. But as time went on there was at least one synagogue in New York for each of these groups.

Just as in Europe the synagogue was for many years the

center of Jewish life, for there were no other Jewish institutions in the community. The stranger came to the synagogue, often for a loan to help him get established in some business, always for the advice and companionship he needed to begin life in new surroundings. There were visits from scholars and rabbis who travelled from land to land to collect funds for Palestine. The wife of a deceased member might need assistance from the congregation to keep a roof over the heads of her young children; a very old member, no longer able to work, must be supported lest he become dependent on the charity of non-Jews.

With the growing Jewish population it became necessary to form various groups outside of the synagogue. Some were designed for "mutual aid"; the members paid dues to care for any of the organization who might need assistance and were assured of help for themselves whenever necessary. Other societies were organized for purely philanthropic purposes, such as hospitals and homes for orphans and the aged. A number of these projects developed into the splendid institutions of our own day.

Like Jewish philanthropy Jewish social life in the early days centered in the synagogue. Jews often mingled with their Gentile neighbors for merrymakings or study or fraternal organizations like the Masons. There were always family gatherings to celebrate a bar mitzvah or a betrothal. But as in Europe the Holy Days meant a community celebration in the synagogue.

An old record book of a New York synagogue mentions a gathering for the traditional night of study on Shabuoth. Lest anyone grow too hungry by midnight the trustees thoughtfully purchased one barrel of "small beer," four shillings worth of crackers and four shillings worth of apples.

A synagogue celebration which was usually attended by many non-members was the ceremony of consecrating the new building. There were prayers and chanting, the lighting of the Ner Tomid (Everlasting Light), the seven-times repeated procession of those who carried the Holy Scrolls. Often these ceremonies were followed by a long and elaborate public dinner.

EARLY JEWISH SCHOOLS IN NEW YORK CITY

Indulgent parents brought their children to these community celebrations, where they at least enjoyed the refreshments. But since all play and no work makes Jacob a very dull child, indeed, these same parents began very early to consider how they might give their children a good education. We have already mentioned the school building which stood beside the first humble synagogue on Mill Street in lower New York. The Jewish children of that city and the first scattered

Jewish communities were either taught at home or attended synagogue schools.

We must remind ourselves that in colonial times there were no tax-supported schools which were attended by all the children of the community. Parents who could afford it paid a fee to cover tuition. Poor children might be taught as an act of charity; otherwise they grew up without an education. It was impossible for a loyal Jew to send his child to any of these schools. Any instruction he might receive from the New England primer to advanced studies in an academy would be based on Christian belief.

But Jews with their deep love of learning could not allow their children to grow up in ignorance. On the first day of Passover, 1731, Shearith Israel dedicated its school, where along with Hebrew, both Spanish and Portuguese were taught. Later these last two languages were dropped; but it was thought that the students still needed six hours daily—with no summer vacations!—in which to master the "three R's"—reading, riting and rithmetic.

A record of the year 1755 states that the salary of the teacher was a load of fire wood every year while every three months he was to receive a shilling for each pupil who paid tuition. This salary was later increased on condition that he conduct free classes in his own house for poor children. In time six other synagogue schools were established in New York City.

The Constitution which insisted on a sharp separation between Church and State did much to popularize public schools with Jewish parents. Although a number of wealthy Jews still sent their children to boarding schools or had them taught at home by tutors, most Jews preferred that their children should attend public schools, since education was no longer under the control of a state church.

Of course, Jews did not expect that Hebrew and Jewish history would be taught in these secular schools. Many of the synagogue schools, facing a diminishing enrollment, closed; for some years there were no Talmud Torahs to take their place. Some parents arranged for their children—especially boys!—to receive private instruction in Hebrew. But sometimes the family was indifferent or too poor to pay a teacher, and many young people grew up without a Jewish education.

Fortunately, very soon we find the forerunner of our modern religious school beginning in Philadelphia. So let us visit the gracious lady who began it all, Rebecca Gratz, perhaps the best-loved heroine in Jewish American history.

A LOVELY LADY OF PHILADELPHIA

There are two good reasons why Rebecca Gratz became the founder of our modern religious school system. As she lived in Philadelphia, she was well acquainted with the Protestant

Sunday School movement which began there in 1791. It was so successful she wondered how a system of weekly religious instruction might be arranged for Jewish children.

Also she was a member of a family which from its arrival in America was strongly identified with every Jewish cause. Her Uncle Barnard was one of the founders of Mikveh Israel congregation; her father, Michael Gratz, served as its president. One of his twelve children, Hyman, established in Philadelphia a college for Jewish studies which still bears the family's name.

Although all historians agree that Rebecca, like the princess of the old fairy tales, was as good as she was beautiful, some dispute whether certain oft-repeated episodes are sober fact or merely legend. One of the unsolved mysteries is her only love affair and the fact that with all her charm and her social position she never married. The story runs that in her youth she loved a Christian but that his religion reared a barrier between them. Some say that when her lover died Rebecca, who had long ago vowed to remain unmarried for his sake, placed three rosebuds in his coffin.

Then there is the story with which every reader of that exciting romance, *Ivanhoe*, is familiar. Again, we cannot be too certain as we sift fact from fancy; but it seems quite reasonable that Rebecca Gratz was actually the model for the heroine of Walter Scott's well-known tale.

There is plenty of evidence that Washington Irving, the popular author of *Rip Van Winkle, The Legend of Sleepy*

Rebecca Gratz

Hollow and a score of other tales, was a close friend of the Gratz family. During his visits to Philadelphia he often visited the Gratz mansion where, it is said, a certain room was set aside for his bedchamber. As an intimate friend, he surely knew the story of Rebecca's romance which her devotion to her people caused her to end so abruptly; he had many opportunities to observe how she tried to forget her own grief by devoting her life to her family and to various charitable causes.

During a visit to Europe Irving was entertained by Sir Walter Scott, who planned to write a novel of chivalry in the time of Richard the Lionhearted. One of the characters, Scott told the American visitor, was to be a Jewish moneylender, Isaac of York.

"You must give him a lovely daughter," we can hear Irving suggesting. "Let me tell you of a young woman named Rebecca, who is one of the most beautiful belles in all Philadelphia." With the skill of an experienced story teller, Washington Irving told of Rebecca's devotion to her religion, her hopeless love, her life of saintly service.

We are told that shortly after Irving's return to America, he received a copy of the newly published *Ivanhoe*, with a letter in which Scott inquired: "How do you like my Rebecca? Does the Rebecca I have pictured compare well with the pattern given?"

The legend, if it was no more than a legend, spread and was generally believed, because like Scott's heroine the Jewess of Philadelphia was beautiful, charitable and loyal to her people. Rebecca Gratz steadfastly refused to affirm or deny that she had served as a model for the most fascinating Jewess in all English literature. But she began to weaken a little in her old age and usually met the question with a smiling, "They say so, my dear!"

Meanwhile she lived a life which although far less thrilling than the fictional Rebecca was certainly more useful. When her sister died Rebecca Gratz brought up the nine motherless children. In spite of her many domestic duties she always kept in touch through her letters with the absent members of her family and her many friends. After all these years her correspondence still sparkles with the wit and charm which made her so popular in the social circles of her own day.

But she was not content to remain what a contemporary writer called a "queen of society." She gave not only of her wealth but her time and her rare ability as an executive to many causes both Jewish and non-Jewish. One of the latter organizations bore the rather forbidding title of the Female Association for the Relief of Women and Children in Reduced Circumstances. Miss Gratz organized the Female Hebrew Benevolent Society of which she became secretary. She also founded the Philadelphia Orphan Asylum in 1815 and served as a secretary for this badly needed institution for forty years.

But perhaps her most enduring work was in the field of Jewish education. For over a quarter of a century she was the superintendent of the Sunday School which she had founded in her home city.

We said earlier she had been inspired by the first Christian Sunday School in Philadelphia. But, of course, she could not use its text books or follow its curriculum. Rebecca Gratz had no training as an educator; but her deeply religious feelings, her pioneer spirit, and her willingness to work untiringly for a project she believed in, all helped to make her school successful.

There were no text books for the religious education of Jewish children. So Miss Gratz not only planned the lessons to be studied but wrote the lesson outlines she handed to her inexperienced teachers. Later, no matter how busy she might be, she always found time to make copies of these lessons to send to another early Jewish educator in Charleston, South Carolina.

A BRAVE LADY OF THE SOUTH

The schoolmistress who eagerly waited in Charleston for Miss Gratz's letters was Penina Moise, a woman who resembled the Philadelphia Jewess only in her deep devotion to her religion. Miss Gratz was rich and beautiful; Penina Moise was poor and plain of face. But there must have been one good fairy who hovered above her cradle and bestowed on the child the gift denied the great lady of Philadelphia—the gift of song.

It is fortunate that it is not necessary to have a formal education in order to write poetry, for the girl had practically no schooling.

Shortly after the close of the Revolutionary War the Moise family, which was of French origin, were driven from their home on the island of San Domingo in the West Indies. A terrible slave uprising had not only robbed them of most of their possessions but had threatened their lives.

Abraham Moise found shelter for his family in Charleston, where Penina, one of nine children, was born. Until she was twelve she lived a happy, normal life, romping with her brothers and sisters through the rambling, comfortable house, and spending blissful hours with her favorite story books. But shortly after her twelfth birthday, Penina's father died and uncertainty and hardship descended on the family.

Mr. Moise's death left his widow and children to face dire poverty. The older children found work and tried to support the family. Penina was now old enough to attend classes in one of the Finishing Schools for Young Ladies so popular in that day. But even if some family friend had paid her tuition, the proud, shabbily dressed girl would have shrunk from associating with the daughters of the rich. And she could not be spared from her home where her frail mother expected her to share the household duties.

Now there was little time for reading. Mrs. Moise's condition grew worse and soon she became helplessly paralyzed. Cleaning and cooking and helping to nurse the invalid so crowded Penina's days that often she could not escape to her cherished books until late at night.

Her eyes had never been very strong. Her sight became weakened through working on embroidery and "fine sewing," for her mother was determined that at least this part of a well-brought up young lady's education should not be neglected. Now to save the expense of a candle she often read by moonlight. Her eyes blurred and ached but it was often nearly midnight when she turned the last page. It was as though she felt driven to learn all she could before the darkness descended upon her.

While still in her teens Penina began to write verses which at first she offered timidly for publication. To her surprised delight her poetry was accepted—and sometimes paid for!—by the leading Jewish and non-Jewish papers of her day. Her family were very proud and happy when some of Penina's verses were collected and published in a volume titled, *Fancy's Sketch Book.* She was no longer an unknown household drudge. Some of the most cultured leaders of Charleston read her book and offered her their friendship. They invited her to their "literary teas." Later her own home became the center of Charleston writers and scholars.

When she became the superintendent of the first Sunday School for Charleston's Jewish children, Miss Moise wrote songs and verses for her pupils to sing and recite. She taught Jewish history so vividly that it was no longer a collection of dry dates and the names of kings; every lesson helped the students to realize the dignity and the heroism of their people. But in spite of her Jewish pride and loyalty Penina Moise was never a narrow-minded bigot. She could see good in all religions and had many warm friends who were not of her faith. When a Charleston minister died she, a Jewess, was requested to write a poem in his honor.

In 1854 the scourge of yellow fever struck Charleston. There were no trained nurses in those days; people who had fallen ill had to depend on members of their families to care for them. So many were stricken with the plague that there was a call for volunteers to care for them. Miss Moise had had plenty of nursing experience while caring for her invalid mother. It was easy for her to bring cleanliness and comfort into a neglected sick room; she had learned to obey a physician's orders. In those days little was known concerning the effect of a patient's spirits on his recovery. Miss Moise, sensitive like all true poets, recognized this. She did her best to keep her patients cheerful with jokes and amusing stories. Just to listen to her, they exclaimed gratefully, did them more good than medicine.

She nursed Jew and Christian alike, and if death came she shared the prayers of the dying. She repeated in Hebrew or English the prayers of the synagogue and the church and asked the God of all mankind to be merciful to all of His children.

Penina's only sister had married early and gone to live far from Charleston. Now after thirty years she returned bringing her daughter with her. It was a joyful reunion and the three women began to plan eagerly for the future. Then a second plague descended on Charleston and cut short their happiness. The Civil War brought much suffering to Charleston. As a life-long Southerner Penina remained loyal to her native state. She believed that the young men who left the beautiful old city to face forced marches and imprisonment and even woundings and deaths on the battlefield fought for a righteous cause. She wrote a poem as stirring as a battle cry to encourage these young soldiers.

Beside the war a personal tragedy entered her life. Her eyes had grown weaker and dimmer; they finally darkened forever. Penina Moise met this latest misfortune with her own bright courage. She knew that one of her favorite English poets, John Milton, had while he sat in darkness dictated *Paradise Lost* to his daughters. Not even blindness, she vowed, would make her idle and useless.

She dictated her poetry to her sister, her many friends. Much of it was religious. Some of her hymns were sung in the Charleston synagogue; later they were published in the *Union Hymnal* and are still used in many congregations. In spite of her growing financial troubles, her doubtful health and her darkened eyes, Miss Moise wrote many gay and humorous verses. She still refused to whine over her own troubles.

Penina Moise received pitifully small sums for her poems; what poet was ever well paid? She could not support herself by writing. And her world offered few opportunities to women, even when not handicapped by blindness. But she loved books and young people; perhaps she might earn her living as a teacher.

Miss Moise and her sister opened a private school for girls. She enjoyed teaching; if her pupils learned little else they acquired a gift which is all too rare today. They took turns reading aloud to their teacher; she gently corrected their delivery or explained the meaning of a difficult passage. When the lessons of the day were over and the pupils had bidden her goodby, the children of Penina Moise's many Jewish and Christian friends came to visit her. Often they asked whether they should read to her from the books she knew so well that she could actually turn without a moment's hesitation to the right page.

Some of these young readers remembered all their lives the frail figure in the deep chair beside the bedroom window. She always wore, they said, a cap of sparkling clean muslin; its whiteness was in strong contrast to the black scarf folded about her face to keep off draughts. They recalled, too, how even in her last years she sat with her head held high and her spine stiffly erect, the posture of a Southern lady which she wished to impress upon her pupils.

A frail, pain-wracked woman, lonely for the sister who had gone before her, she faced death as courageously as she had always faced life. For, as she so truly wrote in one of her more familiar hymns:

> In God, the holy, wise and just,
>   From childhood's tender years,
> Have I reposed with perfect trust,
>   My changing hopes and fears.

Penina Moise resembled her more glamorous contemporary in one more respect which we have neglected to mention: they both were over eighty when they died.

Before we leave the Jewish authors of this day, we should make the acquaintance of a very different writer of a slightly earlier period. For he played a gallant although not always a dignified role in our Jewish adventures. Mordecai Manuel Noah, who was considered one of the leading journalists and political figures of his time, often boasted that at the wedding of his parents George Washington stood close to the chuppah (canopy) and later kissed the lovely bride. Mr. Mordecai could not take any credit for the friendliness of a president of the United States; but he liked to brag loudly and often of the honor conferred on his family.

Mordecai's mother died in Charleston before the boy reached his seventh birthday. Shortly afterwards his father disappeared, to become later the hero of one of his romantic son's unbelievable stories. Fortunately for the child, his grandfather of the well-known Phillips family took him to Philadelphia and brought him up as his own son.

It is not known exactly when Mordecai Noah, wishing to be independent, put away his school books and apprenticed himself to a Philadelphia wood carver. He spent his leisure time reading heavy, solid books on his favorite subjects, history and politics; when he felt the need of amusement he joined his young friends in amateur dramatics. He also tried to see every play that was presented at the Chestnut Street Theater; before long he attempted to write plays himself.

Today Mordecai Noah's high-flown melodramas are read only by students of the theater; they are never acted. But once these plays were very popular with Philadelphia and New York audiences for they were written in a dashing, colorful style and usually dealt with some topic of current interest like "The Siege of Tripoli" or "Marian, or the Hero of Lake George." The playwright knew that introducing pirates, who at that time still attacked American merchantmen on the high seas, or reviving romantic memories of the Revolution would always make a play successful. But he sometimes went too far in trying to please his patrons. He really hoped to produce something quite extraordinary when he planned certain effects in his historical drama, "The Grecian Captive, or The Fall of Athens." But the ungrateful audience only laughed.

It was really the elephant's fault!

But let us begin at the beginning. In that day many plays were printed in paper editions. Mr. Noah thought it would be a fine thing if people in the audience had a chance to glance over "The Grecian Captive" before the curtain rose for the first act. So every patron received a little paper pamphlet when he entered the theater. Unfortunately, nearly everyone became so interested in the printed copy that few looked at the stage. When the readers reached the bottom of a page and turned to the next it sounded like a mighty wind rushing through a forest. This disturbed the actors and annoyed the elephant.

Mr. Noah had thought of another device to interest his audience. He was sure that everyone would appreciate the novelty of having the hero-general carried upon the stage on the back of a magnificent elephant.

The elephant, which was borrowed from a local menagerie, was well-trained and appeared to be well-mannered. But just as it stepped upon the stage the audience to a man turned a page. The beast, excited by the unexpected noise, reared so violently that the hero instead of making an impressive entrance flew over its head and landed among the horns and bass viols of the startled orchestra. The audience was not impressed; it howled with laughter.

For days everybody joked and laughed over Mr. Noah's elephant; but he was not troubled for he knew that even ridicule may be used for advertising purposes. Besides he had a keen sense of humor. When he lived in New York City and was appointed sheriff, a political opponent insisted that no Jew should be allowed to hold that position.

"His duties might call for an execution," he explained, "and it would be wrong to allow a Jew to hang a Christian."

Mordecai Noah was ready with his answer. "It would be a fine Christian," he declared, "who deserved hanging!"

He made a very good sheriff, by the way, and won considerable attention, both favorable and unfavorable, by flinging wide the doors of the jail house when the horror of yellow fever stalked through the city.

A man of such forcible character was bound to make both warm friends and violent enemies. When Mordecai Manuel Noah tried his hand at journalism in Charleston, his daring political ideas were expressed in such an intemperate fashion that he received a challenge to a duel. Fortunately for Mr. Noah, who was far more nimble with his pen than his pistol, after four hours of discussion the duel was called off.

Mordecai Noah was greatly relieved, although certain leading politicians of Charleston had promised to bury him "with all the Civil and Military honors." This experience did not teach him caution. He never hesitated to express his opinion; whether right or wrong, his vigorous utterances both on the political platform and in the newspapers he edited were always thought-provoking and brilliantly expressed.

He was aggressive not only as a politician and writer but also as a Jew. He served on the board of Shearith Israel; was the hard working president of New York's Hebrew Benevolent Society; and showed an active interest in many other Jewish organizations and Jewish education. But what makes him stand out so boldly among prominent and devoted Jews of his day was his grandiose plan to build a new Zion for his people.

The plan very likely started in Mordecai Noah's restless mind when President Madison in 1813 sent him to represent this country as consul to Tunis. As the representative of the

United States, Mr. Noah handled the delicate negotiations necessary to ransom Americans taken prisoner by the pirates of the Barbary States. There were equally delicate decisions to be made in the interpretation of treaties between our country and the African governments. As might have been expected, Mordecai Manuel Noah acted with less diplomacy than vigor and he was soon recalled.

He brought back with him a first-hand knowledge of the desperate poverty and persecution under which the Jews of the Near East dragged out their lives. Noah knew that throughout Europe also Jews suffered and sorrowed and prayed for redemption. He was a student of Jewish history and had even written on Jewish subjects. Mr. Noah did not have to be told how passionately these unhappy people desired to return to their never forgotten Homeland.

Mordecai Noah was always impatient; he refused to wait for a miracle. Let God in His own good time redeem His promise to restore the exiles to Palestine, decided Mr. Noah, but meanwhile let them find a happy refuge in America.

Who would be their leader and protector? Mordecai Manuel Noah suggested that because of his experience in American politics he should be the first Governor and Judge over Israel since Biblical days. Since no one cared or dared to oppose his election, he triumphantly assumed the office and went on with the plans that must have seemed to many the dreams of a mad visionary instead of the proposition of a practical politician.

How would the Jews of Europe, Asia and Africa know that a place of refuge awaited them across the seas? Mr. Noah promptly sent proclamations, as enticing as a modern real estate advertisement, to these scattered Jewish communities. To make his invitations absolutely authentic he signed each with his new title, Governor and Judge over Israel.

As a convenient substitute for Palestine, which was then controlled by the Turks, Mr. Noah offered Grand Island across from the small town of Buffalo. This tangled and untamed wilderness covered over 17,000 acres in the Niagara River. We do not know whether the promoter of the scheme invested a dollar of his own in the timber-covered property. Several non-Jews advanced the necessary capital either because they agreed with Mr. Noah that the Jews would be happy as farmers on this fertile soil, or because they thought they had stumbled upon an excellent investment in real estate. These gentlemen were actually offered a chance to make a profit on their investment, but unfortunately they first consulted Mr. Noah. He advised them not to sell "as he had no doubt of the success of his project, which would greatly enhance the value of our lands."

Mr. Noah really believed what he told his backers. He decided that the site was excellent; Jewish farmers could sell their produce by crossing the Niagara River which separated the island Paradise from Buffalo. Buffalo was then hardly more than a village; but Mordecai declared that because of its location it would some day become a rich and crowded city. In this one prediction, at least, the ever optimistic Judge proved a true prophet!

But, asked an over-cautious soul, what about the Indians? If they started to make trouble for the Ghetto-bred Jews—? But we know that Mr. Noah always had his answer. He agreed with certain scholars of his day that the American Indians were "in all probability, the descendants of the lost tribes of Israel, which were carried captive by the King of Assyria." So he invited the Indians to a reunion with their brethren and felt certain that there would be peace between them.

In his letters of invitation to the scattered Jews across the sea Mr. Noah called his still unbuilt city of refuge Ararat. He saw nothing amusing in the name, which he believed was most appropriate. Hadn't Noah of Bible times found a resting place for the Ark on Mt. Ararat? It was a happy coincidence, if nothing more, that the founder of this modern refuge bore the name of Noah!

Noah decided that the time had come to dedicate his dream city. On a bright September day in 1825 the ceremonies began with a long and imposing procession made up of Buffalo's leading citizens; prominent politicians from New York and Philadelphia; Indians gay with feathers; the militia marching smartly in orderly ranks; Mr. Noah's fellow Masons, who sometimes failed to keep step, but looked most imposing in their lodge regalia.

But soldiers and Masons and gaudy Indians were completely eclipsed by the sartorial glories of the Governor and Judge over Israel in his splendid crimson robes trimmed with ermine. Some years before he had received the honorary title of Major; although he had now grown rather portly he still carried himself gallantly and the spectators cheered him again and again.

Marchers and spectators jostled each other as they crowded as close as they could to the little wharf on the Niagara River; all were impatient to embark in the small boats which stood ready to cross to Grand Island. No one became really violent; but there was much shouting and shoving since everyone wanted to be sure to reach the island in time to watch the laying of the cornerstone.

Alas, Mordecai Noah had been kept so busy preparing his speech and trying on his Judge's robe and assuring his Christian friends that Ararat would welcome not only Jews but those of every religion that he had never once considered one important detail. There were not nearly enough boats to take the yelling, pushing crowd across the river. Everybody was sadly disappointed; Mr. Noah most of all. For, so the story

goes, he had never set foot on Grand Island himself and was most anxious to see the site of his City of Refuge with his own eyes.

A hurried consultation among the authorities followed. The band began to play again; the townspeople and Indians, the Masons and politicians and, of course, Mr. Noah marched to St. Paul's Episcopal Church. Because it was the largest building in Buffalo, the friendly rector had offered it for the dedication ceremony. The cornerstone with its carefully worded inscription was displayed; there were readings from the Prophets and Psalms, one in Hebrew; the Benediction. Mr. Noah spoke with great eloquence—and at some length. The militia furnished a welcome ending to the celebration with a salute of twenty-four guns. All in all, the dedication of the still to be built city of Ararat had been a huge success.

There is no record that a single Jew ever came to New York State for the purpose of settling in Ararat. The many who crossed the sea to make a home in the United States were too suspicious of Mr. Noah's romantic schemes to accept his hospitality on Grand Island. Those who continued to suffer privation in other lands still turned their faces to Zion as they prayed. They felt certain that in God's good time they would be permitted to return to Jerusalem.

Nor has anyone ever heard of a single Indian who cared to accept Mr. Noah's invitation to settle on the banks of the Niagara River. The red men had learned to be suspicious of the white intruders; since Mr. Noah was white they decided they had no reason to trust him or his friendly offers.

Twenty years after the cornerstone had been exhibited in the little Buffalo church, Mr. Noah published one of his many pamphlets. Theodor Herzl who was destined to lead the return to Palestine was still unborn. But Mordecai Noah in 1845 anticipated a number of the ideas of the founder of modern Zionism. Fifty years before the beginning of the movement, the man who had dared to call himself Governor and Judge of Israel wrote that he was convinced of the practicability of the return of the Jewish people to the ancient Homeland.

Had Mordecai Noah forgotten the cornerstone which was to mark the beginning of a city never builded? And if he remembered did he try to justify his early mistake? Or did he silently grieve that the dearest project of his life was destined to remain a dream?

We do not know. We know only that today we still have the visible memorial of Mordecai Manuel Noah's generous hopes. It stands today among the many exhibits of the Buffalo Historical Society. If you are interested, you can easily decipher the inscription, composed with such high faith by the lover of his people:

Shema Yisroel, Adonai Elohenu, Adonai Echod. Ararat, a City of Refuge for the Jews, Founded by Mordecai Manuel Noah in the month of Tizri, 5586, Sept., 1825, in the fiftieth year of American Independence.

FROM CABIN BOY TO COMMODORE

From Mordecai Manuel Noah, a man who fought so valiantly with his pen, let us turn to a gallant gentleman who
showed himself just as ready with his sword. For Uriah Phillips
Levy was always the warrior rather than the scholar or debator.
But he resembled the fiery journalist in a number of ways;
he was quick-tempered, he was brave, and he was always
ready to defend the Jewish name.

At the age of ten, Uriah left his Philadelphia home and did
what every boy dreams of doing—went to sea. With this early
start as a cabin boy and his interest in navigation, it is not at
all surprising to find him at twenty-one the master of his own
vessel, the *George Washington*. Now he experienced the first
real adventure of a life crammed with exciting triumphs and
defeats; his crew mutinied, seized the vessel and made their
master a prisoner.

The mutineers left young Levy stranded on a deserted island.
He sighted and signaled a British ship and was rescued; the
captain urged him to enlist in the British Navy. But Levy
insisted he preferred to remain an American and as soon as he
could returned to the United States.

An old record tells us that Uriah Levy tracked down the
criminals who had mutinied against him. He refrained from
inflicting vengeance on the men who had wronged him and

delivered them safely to the proper authorities for punishment. One could hardly expect such cool-headed action from a young man with Levy's violent impulses; but even at the beginning of his career we find the respect for law and justice which characterized his entire life.

The War of 1812 gave him his first real opportunity to distinguish himself in the navy. He volunteered, received a commission as sailing master and soon won recognition by capturing several British vessels. Next we find him in England, where he remained for over a year as a prisoner of war.

Although he rose rapidly in rank, his years in the navy were far from untroubled. Some of his friends believed that Uriah's frequent quarrels with his brother officers were due entirely to their jealousy of one who had served as a cabin boy while they received their training at Annapolis. Others declared Levy's troubles grew out of his own impatient temper.

We do not know which was the real reason; but we do know that any branch of the armed forces has always been slow to change. The unfriendly officers may have resented Levy's long and aggressive efforts to induce the navy to abolish its ancient method of disciplining seamen with the lash. Uriah may have remembered his own early trials when as a frightened cabin boy he had often trembled before his brutal superiors. Now an officer himself, he contended that to punish a sailor with a flogging lessened his self respect and lowered his efficiency and morale. In spite of opposition, Uriah Levy con-

111

tinued to fight this shocking custom. When at last he was victorious he said that he wished it might be written on his tombstone that he had fathered the law "for the abolition of corporal punishment in the United States Navy."

There may have been another reason for the dislike of his brother officers which embittered Levy's life as long as he remained in the navy. He himself insisted that their persecution was due to religious prejudice. This seemed to hurt him deeply, not only as a personal injury, but because he believed so heartily in democracy which should make such prejudice impossible. He states this belief in no uncertain terms:

"My parents were Israelites, and I was nurtured in the faith of my ancestors. In deciding to adhere to it, I have exercised but a right guaranteed to me by the Constitution of the United States . . . while claiming this right, I have ever accorded it to all men, and as an officer of the navy, I have treated each and every one as a man and never as a partisan or sectarian."

It is hard to separate Levy's love for democracy from his hero-worshiping regard for Thomas Jefferson, its greatest American defender. If you visit Statuary Hall in the Capitol of Washington you will be sure to notice the statue of Jefferson; but it is not all likely your guide will tell you that it was donated by Uriah P. Levy.

You may travel further south into Virginia, and visit Monticello, the majestic mansion, which President Jefferson designed and where he lived for so many happy years. Again, it is not likely that the guide will tell you that Uriah Levy purchased this home from President Jefferson's heirs. The last owner, Levy's nephew, followed his uncle's wishes. The great domed building with its beautiful lawns and gardens now belongs to the nation, thanks to the generosity of Jews who wished to honor its builder.

But all this happened long after the stormy days when Levy literally fought to preserve his rank and personal honor. Duels were still considered a proper method of settling disputes between gentlemen; Levy was too proud to refuse a chance to vindicate himself. In one of these encounters he killed his opponent.

He had risen to the rank of captain. Now he doggedly faced the agony of a court martial. Six times he was tried and finally reduced in rank. Unable to face his enemies any longer, the unhappy man left the country he had tried so hard to serve. His travels took him to Brazil. There the Emperor offered him an important post in the Brazilian Navy. Levy must have been sorely tempted. But he answered that he felt he could never accept a position under a foreign government.

The story of Uriah Phillips Levy has a happy ending. When he returned to the United States, a congressional committee cleared him of the charges which had been brought against him. His captaincy was restored to him. Later he received another promotion which gave him the rank of Commodore, the highest rank in the United States Navy at that time.

THE GENEROUS GENTLEMAN OF NEW ORLEANS

Now we will spend a few minutes with a gentleman who was neither a writer nor naval officer. Just a plain shopkeeper! he would have described himself had a stranger asked him his occupation. Yet this modest business man, Judah Touro, did far more to win respect for his people than the flamboyant Mr. Noah or the quarrelsome Commodore Levy.

Judah Touro was born in Newport on a day which brought both grief and glory to our country, the day when its untried defenders died on Bunker Hill and by their example encouraged other patriots to carry on the fight. Curiously enough, it is in connection with the battle on Bunker Hill that the name of Judah Touro first became known and venerated through the United States.

It was in the year 1843; a group of citizens which had long tried to raise a memorial to the heroes of Bunker Hill now confessed it seemed impossible to collect the required sum. A wealthy Bostonian responded with the offer of ten thousand dollars. Then from far-off New Orleans came a promise to donate an equal amount. Inspired by these princely gifts, the committee resumed its work of collecting funds and the rest of the money was soon raised.

At the dedication ceremonies one of the speakers read a poem which gave special praise and thanks to the two most

114

generous donors. Many in the audience were far more familiar with the Bible than we are today and appreciated these lines:

Amos and Judah—venerated names!
Patriarch and prophet press their equal claims . . .
Christian and Jew, they carry out a plan—
For though of different faith, each is in heart a man.

The Amos who bore a prophet's name was Amos Lawrence of Boston; the "patriarch" was Judah Touro.

During his New England boyhood, Judah could never have dreamed that one day his donation to the Bunker Hill Monument would be reckoned among many other equally generous donations. His father, cantor of the Newport synagogue, died when Judah was ten years old, his mother when he was twelve. Judah's uncle, Moses Michael Hays, a wealthy merchant in Boston, brought the orphan up in his own home and gave the lad the meager education which was considered sufficient at that time.

Later Mr. Hays took his nephew into his counting house and thoroughly trained him for a business career. Sometimes it is thought that Judah left Boston because of his unhappy love for his cousin Catherine Hays. Since no one has ever discovered any other bar to their marriage, it is probable that their romance ended because Mr. Hays believed that cousins should not marry. But there is no prohibition in Jewish law against the marriage of cousins and we can only wonder why the Boston merchant separated the lovers. It may well be that their love continued through their entire lives for neither ever married.

Judah Touro was in his middle twenties when he left Boston forever and journeyed to New Orleans. Why did he not return at least for a visit to his relatives and many old friends? A very simple and unromantic reason strikes us as quite convincing. On the long and tedious sea voyage to Louisiana Touro is said to have suffered so severely from seasickness that he vowed never to risk another trip by water. He seems to have had no great love for adventure; so it is likely he shrank from the lengthy and often dangerous land journey back to his boyhood home.

Can't you see him as he left the sailing vessel, which for so long had been his hated tossing prison? One pictures him as a slender, almost delicate youth with serious eyes. It is not likely he was excited over the prospect of making his fortune in a strange land; probably young Touro even at the wharf was already quietly considering how he could best attract customers to the little shop he meant to open as soon as he could find just the right location.

The young man from Boston landed in New Orleans a year before President Thomas Jefferson had astounded the whole nation by purchasing the great tract of Louisiana from Emperor Napoleon. During the time Touro set himself up as

116

Judah Touro Landing at New Orleans

a shopkeeper, the little city at the mouth of the Mississippi was
still a French colonial possession. The majority of the inhabitants were French who spoke the language of their forefathers;
nearly all of them were Catholics. Other citizens were Spaniards, also Catholics; but there were some Protestants like

117

young Mr. Rezin Davis Shepherd, a "foreigner from Virginia" who soon became Judah Touro's closest friend.

It was fortunate that Judah Touro could depend on Shepherd for companionship for in those first years in New Orleans the Jew from New England must have felt rather shy among so many strangers. The lively French and Creoles, the grave, romantic-looking Spaniards, the Negro slaves, and even the few "Yankees" who had drifted in from "up North" were all so different from the folk of Boston and Newport. Many of the citizens of New Orleans had never known a Jew before they met Touro. He must have quickly overcome any feelings of prejudice or distrust they may have entertained, for soon they flocked to his little store and began to treat him as one of themselves.

They may have been won over by his warm friendliness and his scrupulous honesty. Also, although few tried to imitate this trait, his customers surely admired his brisk New England efficiency. The goods his old friends sent him from Eastern ports were always kept in the neatest possible order; if he promised to have an article by a certain date the purchaser was never disappointed.

Mr. Touro, said his admirers, never seemed to care to take his ease like a Southern gentleman. He never trusted his affairs to slovenly clerks. No matter how great his wealth he was the first person in his shop every morning. Yes, he came to open the shutters, always to the minute; people whose houses he passed on the way used to set their watches by him! Or they sometimes waited until evening, when, after lingering until the last clerk had left, Mr. Touro carefully closed the tall green shutters and, always at precisely the same minute, walked slowly home to supper and to bed.

A business tended so carefully was sure to expand. At first Touro's profits from his imported goods were small. But he invested his capital in ships and in real estate in the rapidly growing city. His shrewd investments brought him larger and larger returns which he wisely reinvested.

Only once in all the fifty years he tended shop in New Orleans did Judah Touro desert his business duties. In 1815 the tumult of this country's second war with England filled the twisted, narrow streets of the sleepy city. General Andrew Jackson arrived with the straight-shooting backwoods men whom he had lately bullied into becoming a well-trained army. But New Orleans was in the gravest danger from the approaching British; not only the city militia but many untrained volunteers were needed. Judah Touro, for once the man of action, offered his services to his country.

General Jackson's army was victorious, but many a hero failed to return to the city he had helped to defend. Judah Touro's one great adventure almost cost him his life. Because he lacked military training he had been given the unskilled but dangerous job of carrying ammunition to the front lines under the guns of the British artillery forces. A heavy shot struck him in the thigh; he fell to the ground, bleeding profusely and unconscious.

A few moments later, another volunteer, Rezin Shepherd, found a field surgeon bending over the stricken man. The doctor shook his head.

"Hopeless!" he told the frantic man. "I will bind his wounds, but I am sure he will never live to reach the hospital.'

Again and again while Mr. Shepherd remained modestly silent, Mr. Touro delighted to tell how his friend had managed to secure a small cart and hurry him to the hospital. It was to such speedy and devoted action, Judah Touro declared, that he owed his life. No wonder the two men, now business partners in many successful enterprises, continued to be the most devoted of friends.

Not only New Orleans, which Judah Touro had soon learned to consider his true home, knew his bounty. You have heard of his interest in the Bunker Hill memorial. No man ever took more pleasure in sharing his wealth. Those who knew him best praised him not only for his princely gifts but his many acts of personal kindness.

Instead of waiting for an appeal to reach him, they said, he actually searched out the unfortunates who needed his help. The Negro slave he educated to be self-supporting and sent away to live in freedom and dignity; the business competitor who needed but was too proud to ask for a loan; the aged widow who shrank from entering the almhouse: to these and a hundred more Judah Touro extended the helping hand of brotherhood.

For the first few years of his life in New Orleans there were only a few Jews in the city. Even when the Jewish population grew, Mr. Touro made no distinction between his own people and those who professed another religion. He was a warm friend of Rev. Theodore Clapp, a New Orleans minister, and was happy to furnish him proof of his friendship. When Mr. Clapp's church burned to the ground, the minister received little sympathy and no material aid from the city's many Catholics as they considered him a heretic. The Protestant congregations were just as unfriendly; none of their members approved of the Rev. Mr. Clapp's teachings because he represented the Unitarian group, at that time most unpopular in the South.

We are shocked to read in a contemporary account that no church "would open its door to Clapp and his congregation for fear of seeming to countenance heresy, but the noble-hearted Jew, Touro, came to the rescue. He purchased a small chapel on St. Charles Street for the congregation to use without charge, until an adequate new structure could be erected."

In our own day, with so many organizations working for better understanding between people of all creeds and races, this may seem a praiseworthy but not a remarkable gesture of friendliness. But in the year 1822 when Judah Touro first lent his Christian friend a large sum to carry on his religious work it was thought so unusual that it was actually mentioned in the Maryland House of Delegates.

This Unitarian clergyman also received a very generous legacy in Judah Touro's will. The many large bequests in this testament bear witness that the poor orphan boy died at seventy-nine a very wealthy man. The individuals remembered were both Jewish and non-Jewish; while the many institutions which were mentioned were of all types—Jewish and Christian and non-sectarian, and situated in cities as far apart as New Orleans and Newport.

He left five thousand dollars to the Hebrew Foreign Mission Society and an equal sum to St. Mary's Catholic Boys Asylum. There were large legacies to two very different local institutions, the Firemen's Charitable Association and the Seaman's Home; for although Mr. Touro had long hated the sea he was always interested in the welfare of the men who served on his ships. We know that he must have continued to love the city of his birth, for the will mentions legacies for a city park, the historic round tower and the Redwood Library of which he had long been an honorary member.

Of course, Judah Touro could not forget the Newport synagogue where his father had chanted services for the pre-Revolutionary congregation. "I give and bequeath Ten Thousand dollars for the purpose of paying the salary of a Reader or Minister . . . and to keep in repair and embellish the

Jewish Cemetery." He had already stated that he desired to be buried where his mother and so many friends of long ago were already sleeping their last sleep.

It would take far too long even to list all of the Jewish causes mentioned in the testament; they ranged from certain philanthropic groups in New Orleans to "the Jews Hospital Society of the City and State of New York Twenty Thousand Dollars" to "the North American Relief Society for the Indigent Jews of Jerusalem, Palestine." Many of the organizations mentioned by the philanthropist were desperately in need of funds at this time; in some cases Mr. Touro's liberal legacies helped worth-while institutions to become firmly established that they might continue even to our own day.

A remarkable feature of this remarkable will is the number of synagogues named. It is no surprise that Mr. Touro, a deeply religious man, left a considerable amount of money to every synagogue which he knew existed in the United States in 1854. The surprise lies in the great growth of Jewish congregations since there were only six in the whole United States at the beginning of President Washington's administration.

But when Mr. Touro died there were synagogues located not only in the largest cities but in smaller communities like Albany and Buffalo and Baltimore, Louisville, Cincinnati and Cleveland. We are awed when we discover that even in one man's lifetime our people could have grown numerous and wealthy enough to furnish such a record.

Many of these outlying groups began with one bold pioneering spirit. Like Jacob Barsimson in 1654! And we have just watched the career of friendly, big-hearted Judah Touro, one of the first if not the very first Jew to make his way in the quaint French city of New Orleans. For Jews seem to have the faculty of springing up in unexpected places at a time when you would never dream of searching for them. (The next time you sing "The Star Spangled Banner" be sure to tell the world that Fort McHenry, which inspired the anthem, numbered eight Jews among its defenders against the British fleet!)

It is not likely that any of you have ever heard of the first white man to live on the present site of Montgomery, Alabama. Well, one day in 1789 when the Indians and the creatures they hunted roamed in that section, an adventuresome Jew came to live there. Abram Mordecai had traveled far and wide since he left his native Pennsylvania. He loved the wilderness and the free life of the red men; he had broken so completely with the ways of his boyhood that he had taken an Indian woman to be his wife.

But although Mordecai was content to follow the half-civilized life of his neighbors, he was not without ambition. He still remembered with pride that he had once served under George Washington. Perhaps the memory sometimes prodded him to ask himself: How can I, the son of a respected Jewish family, one of General Washington's veterans, be satisfied to spend my days bargaining with the Indians for pelties? This wilderness is a part of the America I fought for. I would like to have a share in building my country.

So Mordecai told his long range plans to the Indian agent for the government, Colonel Hawkins, when they met at Pole Cat Springs, Alabama, in 1804. To conquer the wilderness, urged Mordecai, it would be necessary to introduce some industry which would attract permanent white settlers, not roving hunters and traders. What about a cotton gin? The squaws for miles around could be taught to raise cotton which would then be carried down the river in canoes. A gin furnished by the government would prepare the cotton before it was loaded on barges for the New Orleans market.

Colonel Hawkins was delighted with the idea. But the agent warned Mordecai—who most likely knew the Hickory Ground Indians far better than an occasional visitor ever could!—that there might be trouble. There was. Shortly after the first cotton gin in the state of Alabama was erected, Chief Towerculla, who hated this sign of progress in his domain, arrived on the scene with a band of his followers. They wrecked the gin and beat Abram Mordecai so brutally that he barely escaped with his life.

There is no record where the Jew from Pennsylvania roamed in his disappointment; no one seems to know what adventures came to him in his later years. If at the end he wandered back to his long-deserted cabin, he must have grieved to find a thriving settlement called Dudlyville near the spot where he had erected the first cotton gin in the region. For although Abram Mordecai believed in progress, the backwoodsman in him dreaded to see that civilization had conquered the wilderness.

TO CHICAGO AND POINTS WEST

Shall we travel west in a covered wagon to linger for a while in the settlement on the shores of Lake Michigan? As early as 1847 we will find a congregation in Chicago appropriately named Kehillath Anshe Maariv, (Men of the West). When a synagogue was built it served not only the Jews of Chicago but became a religious center for our people from all over the state. As a child I heard my grandfather tell how every autumn he closed his general store in the village of Mendota, Illinois, and traveled eighty miles to attend the Holy Day services at Kehillath Anshe Maariv.

Suppose we leave early Chicago and travel westward, on, on toward the setting sun. If you are a girl you will probably be stowed somewhere in the long wagon which is cluttered with household goods and food supplies. Though if your mother is tired and you are old enough to be trusted with the reins, you may climb upon the high front seat behind the slow-moving but sure-footed oxen. Your older brothers if they are lucky enough to have horses of their own will ride with your father beside the wagon; the little fellows will be distributed among the feather beds in the rear.

A JEW WHO BELIEVED IN TEXAS

Let us pretend we are among the covered wagon folk who on a day in early spring cross the flower-sprinkled plains of Texas. One of our scouts, a useful man wise in the matter of trails and hostile Indians, loves to tell us stories of even earlier pioneers of the western world. As we rest around our camp fire after the day's trek we are surprised to hear him introduce his hero:

"A tenderfoot from over in Europe and a Jew! But everybody in Texas, border to border, is ready to take his hat off to Henry Castro."

There are many legends and the usual Texas "long stories" in our scout's tale. So it may be better for us to repeat only the sober facts.

Henry Castro was born in France in 1786 and first visited Texas when that far-flung expanse was still an independent republic. The flag with its one challenging star still flew over Texas when this foreign Jew first traveled through this section of the West and fell in love with its vastness and its vigor. Castro was past his middle years when he met Sam Houston, the pioneer hero. But the Jew from France was still young in his enthusiasm. Houston believed with all his heart in the growth of Texas; as he told his dreams of the future, his listener could see the plains already dotted with farmhouses and schools and churches. A good land, a rich land, but idle, Castro decided. All it needed was immigrants.

Henry Castro was a very rich man who could afford to pay for the dream which Sam Houston had dreamed. Between the years 1842-1846 he spent $150,000 to bring 5,000 colonists across the sea to the Texas country. Returning to Europe he selected from Alsace and the Rhineland these future builders of the state of Texas. He paid not only for their passage across the Atlantic but took care of their expenses until they were able to support themselves in their new homes.

When in 1861 Castro returned to the United States from his last trip to Europe, he was unable to enter any Northern port, since Texas had chosen to fight for the Confederacy. So Henry Castro tried to travel by way of Mexico to the spot he now considered his home. The difficulties he met on the way proved too severe for a man of seventy-five. His great adventure ended suddenly and he died among strangers in the strange land of Mexico. It would have made him happier could he have known that in years to come a Texas city and county would by their names keep his memory alive.

THE PAINTER WHO CROSSED THE ROCKIES

About ten years before the sound and fury of the Civil War filled the country another Jewish adventurer turned his face to the West. Solomon Nunez Carvalho was born in Charleston; here he turned at an early age to painting and won a prize for his picture, "The Intercession of Moses for Israel." The artist later lived in Philadelphia, Baltimore and New York, where he painted and practised the still primitive craft of photography.

He had always greatly admired dashing John Charles Fremont, equally well-known as a radical politician and explorer of the West. When Fremont in 1853 prepared to make his fifth trip across the Rocky Mountains, Carvalho eagerly accepted his invitation to accompany the party to make daguereotype photographs. He left his wife and young family in Philadelphia to become the first official photographer in the United States to accompany a scientific expedition. Some historians believe that Solomon Carvalho was also the first Jew to cross the Rockies. Others deny him this distinction; they claim that Emanuel Lazarus, who was one of an exploring party of seventeen white men to enter California from the East in 1826, deserves the honor. But there is no definite proof that Lazarus was a Jew.

At all events, Carvalho made the most of his opportunities. He kept a careful record of the hardships suffered by the twenty-two men of the expedition party as in the winter cold they crossed the Rockies on foot. Later he described his experiences in his book: "Incidents of Travel and Adventure in the

Solomon Carvalho with Colonel Fremont

Far West with Col. Fremont's Last Expedition, Across the Rocky Mountains: Including Three Months' Residence in Utah, and a Perilous Trip Across the Great American Desert to the Pacific." This work, which was published in New York in 1857, is the only account of the expedition that survives and is of the greatest value to the historians of the early West.

Aside from its historical and scientific value, Carvalho's book is fascinating to the lover of travel books and adventure stories. We watch him painting portraits of the much discussed First Families of Mormon Utah. Or, at Colonel Fremont's suggestion, the author displays his marksmanship to impress some unfriendly Indians. Carvalho adds that he traded them blankets for three or four apparently healthy horses—which in a few days turned lame and utterly useless.

We read of the crossing of the Grand River, the Eastern fork of the Colorado. The water was six feet deep; at the crossing the roaring current reached the necks of the frightened horses; "the greater portion of their riders' bodies were also immersed in the freezing current . . . my clothes froze stiff on me when I came out of it. . . . It is most singular, that with all the exposure that I was subjected to on this journey, I never took the slightest cold, either in my head or on my chest; I do not recollect even sneezing. While at home, I ever was most susceptible to cold."

Later it became necessary to kill the horses for food. "The

sacrifice of my own pony that had carried me so bravely in my first buffalo hunt, was made; he had been running loose for a week unable to bear even a bundle of blankets. It was a solemn event with me."

In the midst of the icy mountains Carvalho finds comfort in recalling a Hebrew psalm he had learned as a boy in Charleston: "They wandered in the wilderness in a solitary way: They found no city to dwell in. . . . Then they cried unto the Lord in their trouble, and he *delivered them* out of their distresses."

At the end of the trek the men were without shoes. "Some had rawhide strapped round their feet, while others were half covered with worn out stockings and moccasins; Col. Fremont's moccasins were worn out, and he was no better off than any of us."

The reader has a sense of personal deliverance when Carvalho thrusts his hand under the snow, feels the ruts caused by recent wagon wheels and realizes that the road leads to the safety of a settlement. Here the whites mistook him for an Indian, for his hair had not been combed for a month, his emaciated face was filthy and his clothes tattered from hunting game in the brush. His hands were badly frost-bitten; he suffered from scurvy. His privations had left him so low in spirits that when a settler took him into his cabin and the adventurer saw "three beautiful children, . . . I wept for joy to think I might yet be restored to embrace my own."

In the end Solomon Carvalho did return to his family. He spent the rest of his life in his comfortable home in Baltimore and New York City where he worked as artist and photographer. It is likely he still yearned for adventure. Fortunately he was able to occupy his restless mind with certain inventions to improve the heating apparatus of his day. He was so successful that before he died he was made president of the Carvalho Heating and Super-Heating Company.

He seems to have been happy in his family life; as a loyal Jew he must have found satisfaction in working for a number of Jewish causes. He continued his earlier studies in philosophy. Yet more and more as he grew older he regretted that it was now too late for him to seek new frontiers beyond the mountains.

A JEWISH BUILDER IN COLORADO

While we are in the still undeveloped West, why not track down Otto Mears, a Jewish pioneer in Colorado who is well worth our knowing? Once an Indian trader, he has been appointed Indian Commissioner and President Grant is well pleased with the treaty his representative has just signed with the Ute tribe. Otto Mears, who knew service under good old Kit Carson, gets on very well with the long exploited Indians. He knows their language although he speaks it with a thick

Yiddish accent. The Indians never seem to mind. They know that Commissioner Mears is the first white man they have ever met who has not tried to cheat them; they trust him and would be glad to welcome him into the Ute tribe, thus making him the first authentic Jewish Indian on record.

You see, Otto Mears, who was born in Courland of mixed English and Russian Jewish parentage, brought his accent along when as a boy of nine he accompanied his elders to the United States. The family were caught in the excitement of the early days of the Gold Rush and made their way as quickly as they could to California. Boys of the mining camps soon developed into men; by the time Otto was eleven he was quite capable of taking care of himself.

As a young man he fought in the first regiment California sent to help win the Civil War. At the end of the war he drifted to the fertile San Luis Valley in Colorado. One of the earliest settlers, he soon became interested in introducing efficient methods of agriculture into that region, like that Jewish pioneer, Abram Mordecai with the first cotton gin in Alabama! Soon we find him publishing a newspaper and building some of the most important highways and toll roads in Colorado. Ten years after the war he negotiates the treaty with the Utes by which they cede their Colorado lands to the government.

Land cleared of the Indians meant increased immigration, the coming of settlers more dependable and .productive than the trapper or fur trader or miner. But the day of the covered wagons was past. With his own eyes Otto Mears had seen the Iron Horse puffing and snorting across the trackless plains; he may have smiled, though a little sadly, to see the simple Indians tug at their ponies' bridles as they prepared to flee before the unfamiliar monster. Yes, he decided, if we want more folks from the East to settle in Colorado, we've got to build railroads to bring them.

Railroad tracks through the terrific heights of the mountain passes? Engineers and surveyors insisted it couldn't be done. But Otto Mears with his bulldog stubbornness refused to be discouraged. He made up his mind to give Colorado its transportation system and he defied the experts to stop him. It was a long, hard struggle for there were few to share his burdens.

Today in the city of Denver the visitor usually goes first to the State Capitol which the pioneer from Russia supervised during its construction. He will never be forgotten by the grateful citizens of Colorado. For on one of the walls hangs a stained glass portrait of the father of the state's railroad system, the Jew who helped to conquer the Western wilderness.

GOLD—AND JEWS—IN CALIFORNIA

James Marshall, a humble unknown man before that day, which brought evil to many and great wealth to a few, found a bit of shining metal. Gold! he muttered and tried to keep his discovery a secret. But soon everyone for miles around Sutter's mill on California's American River repeated the magic word. Marshall's name became known throughout the state; letters and newspapers carried it and the story of his discovery to bustling New York and New Orleans, drowsy with the summer sun.

Clerks, never pausing to return to the shelf the bolts of silk and cashmere they had been displaying, rushed from their shops to borrow money for a "Western outfit"; in New England villages old men and young men, fathers and sons, gathered around the cracker barrel to discuss ways and means of reaching the new Eldorado; then hastened home to persuade a doubtful wife or mother that she could care for the farm alone. Teachers deserted their schoolrooms; "gentlemen of leisure," whose white hands had never lifted anything heavier than a malacca walking stick, asked each other whether it would be wiser to buy their picks and high boots at once or wait until they reached the coast.

Some of the gold seekers followed the buffalo trails across the plains and mountains. Some who came by water hoped to shorten their journey by disembarking at the Isthmus and tramping through the fever-haunted jungles. Others took passage at New York and sailed around Cape Horn to San Francisco. Soon the harbor was dotted with noble vessels which were left to rot by their deserting crews. Return home with your ship? Never! See you in the gold fields!

The settlement on San Francisco Bay seemed to grow into a straggling city over night. Above the muddy lanes sprang hideous rows of makeshift wooden buildings: saloons, eating houses, shops displaying supplies for miners. Buying, quarreling, drinking, everyone seemed too busy to turn his eyes to the lovely blue waters of the bay and the misty mountains beyond. But sometimes a man might glance toward Telegraph Hill. When he saw the familiar wooden signal swinging above it, he would shriek: "A ship!" In a few minutes the streets and shops would be deserted. From the water's edge the crowd watched impatiently for still another ship to enter the crowded harbor.

Day after day the gold seekers came from every land. Adventurers from China and Australia, from the vineyards of France and the slums of London; men of every race, black and white and yellow; of every creed and with every political belief. The clergyman and the professional gambler; Lola Montez, the dancer for whom a king had lost his throne, and Lotta Crabtree, the child actress, met and became warm friends in the democracy of the mining camps.

Of course, there were Jews among even the earliest groups of the gold-seeking adventurers. The record tells us that there were Jews aboard the first Pacific mail steamer which dropped anchor in San Francisco Harbor in February 1849.

In the same year two groups, which must have aggregated at least twenty worshippers, held Yom Kippur services, one in a tent, the other in a cramped room above a store. On that sacred day those whose parents lived in Poland or England formed the nucleus of San Francisco's congregation, Shearith Israel, still one of the most important congregations in the entire West. The other little band, which seems to have been made up of "Germans and other Jews" became at the same time the founders of Emanu El. The name was of good omen; God was with the worshippers that Yom Kippur and continued to bless them. Today they are housed in a synagogue deservedly famous for its stately and unique beauty. Few California Jews are bold enough to affirm which synagogue is really the older; present day congregants like all San Franciscans are rather touchy in such delicate matters!

There are practically no records of Jews in the "diggings" during the gold rush. No Jews among the gold seekers spent fabulous fortunes to erect the monstrous mansions on San Francisco's Nob Hill. But here and there in little California towns like Marysville and Fiddletown and Shasta, nestled in the shadow of its purple mountain, a Jewish oldster may be coaxed into telling stories of his grandfather who kept a store to supply the miners' needs.

Some of those who came in the lumbering wagons or the crowded ships to seek gold and high adventure remained long after the mines were deserted. We find their names on the crumbling tombstones in the Jewish cemeteries which are scattered through the Pacific states. For here as in the East there was usually the same order: a plot of ground for the first Jewish dead; an organization to care for the unfortunates among the living; and if the Jewish community grew to support one, at last a synagogue and a religious school for the congregation's children.

Among the many Jews whose names are still remembered by every Californian we have space for only two: one a builder of dreams, the other a builder of tunnels and museums and a notable library. We must turn first to Joshua Abraham Norton for in his later days he insisted strictly on royal etiquette and royalty must never be kept waiting!

THE JEW WHO BECAME AN EMPEROR

Of course he really wasn't an Emperor! His parents were just ordinary middle-class English Jews who took their little son to live in Africa's Cape Colony. At an early age Joshua Norton, as he still called himself, set up a business first in Capetown, later in Rio de Janiero. The South American venture must have prospered for when Norton left Brazil he carried with him a considerable fortune. This he expected to double on the Pacific coast.

He arrived in California in the heat of the gold rush. Our merchant adventurer had no intention of using the pick and shovel to dig up his fortune. To set up a store in some mining center and invest his profits seemed too slow a method for a man with Joshua Norton's ambitions. He decided to stay in San Francisco; here he was so successful as a commission merchant that in four years he was rumored to be worth two hundred and fifty thousand dollars.

Now came the biggest and last gamble of Norton's business career. He knew that rice was one of the staples of every miner's diet; it was easy to transport, store and cook; it quickly filled the stomach of a hungry man when the day's back-breaking work was over. He visited the produce ships that passed through the Golden Gate and bought up every grain of rice until he had cornered the market.

Prices soared but Norton planned to hold his rice until they rose even higher. But one day he was horrified to learn that two ships loaded with rice had just entered the harbor. Because of the scarcity Norton had planned to set his price at one dollar a pound; now with the market flooded three pounds of rice sold for less than a dime. He had put all his eggs in one basket, as the saying goes, and now they were cracked and worthless.

His fortune disappeared overnight and Mr. Norton dis-

appeared also. About three years later he again walked the streets of San Francisco. Many of his former friends failed to recognize him for now he dressed and acted like a madman. Some said that his business misfortunes had turned his brain. Others insisted that Joshua A. Norton, shrewd as ever, realized that the happy-go-lucky dwellers of the pleasure-loving city would generously reward anybody who amused them.

Every day Emperor Norton I, as he now called himself, strolled down the main streets. He wore a self-designed military uniform; the long blue coat blazed with brass buttons and huge gilt epaulettes, which managed to remain impressive even after they grew tarnished through age and the San Francisco dampness. His towering beaver hat was heightened by plumes held in place by a showy rosette; he carried a curiously carved cane and, as though a second weapon might be needed, he usually fastened a sword to his broad leather belt. He never paid for this regal outfit; it was presented by the County Supervisors after the Emperor had explained that he knew they would never allow him to appear shabbily dressed on the streets of his favorite city.

He continued to favor San Francisco, although he always insisted that Norton I was Emperor of the *entire* United States *and* the Protector of Mexico. He issued proclamations which abolished Congress and the Supreme Court; during the Civil War he decided that the best way to end hostilities would be to dissolve the Union! What seemed to many his most fantastic decree was his order to construct a suspension bridge across San Francisco Bay. In the little French cafés practical engineers ordered another glass of wine and chuckled over the mad Emperor's latest folly. Who could predict that after sixty years another Jewish dreamer would plan and actually build such a bridge?

But even an Emperor needs food and shelter. Although after his return to San Francisco he never attempted to earn his own living, the gaudily dressed Norton I managed to live comfortably although not in royal style. He paid with a fifty-cent piece every night for the rental of a meanly furnished chamber in a rooming house. This was the exact sum he received as taxes from certain amused business men. No one was ever known to refuse to pay. When one financier was absent from his office for eighteen months, the Emperor called to suggest that unpaid taxes displeased him; he collected the nine silver dollars he considered his just payment.

To make sure that he would never lack funds, Emperor Norton ordered a printer to issue fifty-cent bonds in his name. With these he usually paid for a meal in one of his favorite restaurants; often the proprietor would paste the bond in his window to inform the public that his establishment had just been patronized by royalty.

Theater owners invited him to accept a choice seat; he rode without paying his fare on cable cars, river boats and railroads. Once when a new conductor, strangely unaware of the joke, insisted that Emperor Norton either pay or leave the train, the aging man demanded and received an apology from the railway company.

Hardly less famous than their imperial master were his dogs, Bummer and Lazarus. When the Emperor adopted the homeless mongrels they were bedraggled and half-starved. But after they had accepted their daily share of their master's free meals they grew fat and sleek and important. They followed him everywhere—to listen to debates at the Free Culture Lyceum; to share the monarch's inspection of the cadet corps at the University of California. It was rumored that when he alternately attended services at one of the city's synagogues or the cathedral, his two faithful companions curled themselves at his feet and exhibited the dignified decorum to be expected from hounds of the royal kennels.

These visits to various places of worship have never been proved; but it is an authenticated fact that when Bummer departed for dog heaven a San Francisco newspaper carried a five-hundred word obituary, elegantly describing the virtues of the deceased, and bordered in black. For some years Bummer's stuffed remains were shown as the chief attraction of a saloon in the downtown district.

When the Emperor himself died after a prosperous reign of twenty years, many impressive letters were discovered in the pockets of his resplendent uniform. One, according to local legend, came from his fellow ruler, the Czar of all the Russias; another from President Grant congratulated the old pauper on his marriage to the widowed Queen Victoria. These and other messages had been written by local jokesters; now they soberly joined the city-wide demand that their beloved Emperor be given a royal funeral.

Today as you approach the Golden Gate Bridge you may want to stop to read the tribute to its builder, Joseph Baermann Strauss. It is inscribed at the base of the rather impressive statue which San Francisco has erected to honor the designer of "one of man's greatest engineering achievements." Nor is Emperor Norton I forgotten. He often marches in the Thanksgiving Day parade, a swaggering figure in a blue coat and tall beaver hat. Treasure hunts sometimes bear his name and the "Treasure" is stamped with the Emperor's likeness. Best of all a few confectionary stores still sell "Emperor Norton Ice Cream."

Another Jew of pioneer days whom San Francisco still remembers is Adolph Heinrich Joseph Sutro. At first glance one might think that no two men could be so different in character and in achievement. But both dreamed mighty dreams, dared much and were happy in the end.

Sutro, who was born in Prussia, came to the United States in the great German migration of 1848 which we will shortly describe. The family first settled in Baltimore, but lured by stories of the gold rush, the ambitious youth soon joined the excited adventurers who poured into California.

Later he drifted to Nevada where the romance of the Comstock Lode began. The fabulously rich output of the mines was seriously threatened by floods from underground sources. Adolph Sutro, although not an engineer, pondered long and earnestly on some method by which the mines could be saved.

When he was sure he had evolved a practical plan, he organized the Sutro Tunnel Company. The tunnel, which took ten years to build, was four miles long and was blasted sixteen hundred feet below the mountains. It was so constructed that it carried away the water—and the mines were saved.

Adolph Sutro returned to San Francisco a famous man and a millionaire. He believed in the growth of the city and invested his capital in real estate. But although he became one of the richest men in a state where fortunes were made overnight, Sutro remained unspoiled by his sensational success.

He had always loved books; now one of his greatest joys was to add to his private library. At his death it contained over two hundred thousand carefully selected volumes as well as a number of rare Hebrew manuscripts. He also loved gardens and took great delight in the vast grounds of his estate. First he built the dignified white mansion which crowns a high flower-covered cliff beside the Pacific. Next he designed the garden, in which he tried to combine Greek beauty, European folk lore and the luxuriant growth of California. For along some of the garden walks reproductions of classic statues gleam whitely through the shrubs, heavy with blossoms, while here and there peep out brightly colored plaster gnomes which must have reminded the owner of the fairy tales of his German boyhood.

Alfred Sutro owned a tenth of the city's land; he felt he must share his good fortune with San Francisco's citizens. He gave them not only Sutro Park but added a museum and an aquarium to his gift. Although in 1894 San Francisco was not yet one of the large centers of Jewish population, Mr. Sutro was so popular with its citizens that they elected him mayor. His was the oft-repeated tale—the immigrant Jewish boy who plays a worthy part in the American adventure and wins honor for himself and his people.

A few pages back we mentioned that the Sutro family came to the United States during what historians often call the German migration. You may remember that in the earliest days the Sephardim, whose ancestors had been driven from the Spanish peninsula, formed the majority of Jewish immigration. Of course, almost from the beginning there were Jews who migrated from England and Central Europe like Francis Salvador and Haym Salomon.

The German migration included Jewish and non-Jewish emigrants not only from the German states but nearby countries like the Austro-Hungarian Empire. It was a living wave that rose higher and higher with the passing years. Many who came were miserably poor and hoped in America to earn a decent living for themselves and their families. But there were also scholars and writers and physicians who hoped to live a freer life without all the hateful restrictions of their native lands.

Napoleon I had promised and in many cases granted a certain amount of freedom to the oppressed peoples. After his fall in 1814, a cloud of the blackest reaction settled over Europe. The Jews who had dreamed of liberty and equal opportunities once more found themselves crowded behind their stifling ghetto walls.

In Germany and Austria-Hungary, in Italy and in France the spirit of revolution slowly spread. The anger of the discontented people might smolder for years before it burst into flames—quickly stamped out by the armies of the oppressive governments. European Jews even if they were not interested in politics knew what the struggle for human rights meant to them and to their children. The more advanced thinkers among them often joined Gentile liberals in the battle for a new society.

Many intellectuals were so discouraged by the failure of the Revolution of 1848 that they despaired of living a good life in Europe. Among these Forty-Eighters were a number of Jews, who later played an important part in American life. To this group belonged Isaac Mayer Wise, probably the most famous of American rabbis, who felt he could no longer endure the petty anti-Jewish laws of his native Bohemia; and Joseph Brandeis, the father of the first Jew to serve on the Supreme Court. There were Rabbi David Einhorn whom we will meet later as the dauntless opponent of black slavery; the scholarly Rabbi Benjamin Szold, who in his youth had fought against reaction in Vienna.

Nor should we forget Dr. Abraham Jacobi, sometimes called the founder of the science of pediatrics in the United States. Because after his graduation from a German university in 1851 he dared to identify himself with the Revolutionary movement, he was charged with high treason and suffered im-

GROWTH OF JEWISH POPULATION
IN RELATION TO GROWTH OF
UNITED STATES POPULATION

160,000,000

120,000,000

50,000,000

17,000,000

4,000,000

3,000 JEWS
1790

15,000 JEWS
1840

250,000 JEWS
1880

4,200,000 JEWS
1928

5,185,000 JEWS
1954

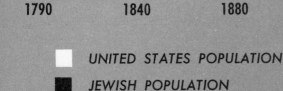

UNITED STATES POPULATION

JEWISH POPULATION

prisonment for three years. As soon as he was released he came to New York City. He died at eighty-nine after contributing much to science as physician, professor in several leading medical colleges, and outstanding researcher in children's diseases.

Of course, not all the German Jews who came to the United States during this period were scholars and scientists. Most of these immigrants were peddlers and small shop keepers. Few were rich, for people who are prosperous in their native countries seldom emigrate. Although they had been far from happy in their former homes, many German Jews on their arrival tried to live in a German neighborhood. This may explain why Cincinnati was one of the earliest of Ohio cities to have a large Jewish population. For from its earliest settlement Cincinnati was so strikingly German that a section across a small drainage canal was designated as "Over the Rhine."

The German Jews of this period, like so many other immigrant groups, joined musical and athletic societies where they could mingle with others "from back home." Since it was easier at first for them to read German than English, several of the early Jewish newspapers in this country were printed in German.

Many of these newcomers knew little Hebrew. Although a number of them remained Orthodox and continued to follow the religious customs of their forefathers, this was the group which welcomed the teaching of Rabbi Isaac M. Wise. In our final section when we study Jewish institutions in the United States, we will learn how Rabbi Wise's ideas differed from Orthodox beliefs.

WAR BETWEEN BROTHERS

In the next decade the Jews of this country were to be as sharply divided in their political as in their religious views.

The question of slavery lowered more and more threateningly between the North and the South. As always, the Jews thought and argued and voted not as a united body but according to their own convictions as independent citizens.

Among Jews as among other Americans opinions on the rights and wrongs of slavery were largely a matter of geography. There were few Jewish slave owners in the South; but a Jew who lived in Virginia or South Carolina or Georgia would be more likely to approve of the familiar institution; he would certainly agree with his Gentile neighbors on the question of state rights. A citizen living in the industrialized North had nothing to lose if slavery were abolished. He was not troubled over the issue of state rights. In many cases like the German Christian immigrants, whose votes kept a doubtful border state like Missouri in the Union, the German Jew felt very strongly on the question of freedom.

Of course there were always a few Jews who opposed slavery even though they lived in the South. You may recall Judah Touro of New Orleans. Isaiah Isaacs of Virginia not only declared that "all men are by nature equally free" but proved his sincerity by leaving directions in his will for the freeing of his slaves.

Rabbi Isaac M. Wise in Cincinnati, a city with many Southern sympathizers, urged in his weekly paper, "The Israelite," that all Jews should remain neutral on this violently discussed issue. He believed that the Jews of the United States were still a small, weak body and could not afford to be torn by political dissensions. But although he was most influential in many other phases of Jewish life, in this matter few of his followers heeded his warning. As the bitterness between the two factions grew, many of Isaac M. Wise's fellow rabbis, even though men of peace, were forced to take a definite stand.

As in the days of the Revolutionary War many turned to the Old Testament to bolster up their own opinions. The Southern orator loved to refer to the story in Genesis when the angel of the Lord bids the slave woman Hagar to return to her master. Didn't that prove that God Himself sanctioned slavery? To which an abolitionist would answer: But aren't we told a little later on in the same Book that God helped the first abolitionist, Moses, to rescue his enslaved people from the land of Egypt!

Often the black slave over whom the statesmen wrangled could not read the Bible for himself, for in some of the Southern states the law forbade anyone to teach him to read or write. But many Methodist and Baptist preachers wandered from plantation to plantation to bring the word of God to the neglected bondmen. The slave listened to the Book the white clergyman carried with him. When the preacher spoke of the Hebrew's Promised Land, the Negroes thought of a land of freedom, perhaps Canada. As they listened to the story of the Exodus from Egypt, they identified Pharaoh with their own taskmasters and defied the tyrant in their spiritual, "Go down, Moses!" No wonder more than one slave owner began to wonder whether the Bible wasn't rather dangerous reading.

In New York City Rabbi Morris J. Raphall preached a sermon which was later printed, widely circulated and violently discussed by Jews and Christians alike. To many he seemed to defend slavery on the ground that it was permitted in Bible days.

Michael Heilprin, a popular Jewish journalist of that day, also knew his Bible. In an article in the "New York Tribune" he eloquently challenged Rabbi Raphall's views. A Polish Jew by birth, Heilprin had taken part in the Revolution of 1848. When he reached the United States he did not have to wait to earn his living with his pen for he already knew English along with a dozen other languages. He loved America dearly, not only because he was able to earn a good income and

153

achieve an enviable reputation as a journalist. He could never forget that this country had granted him the first real freedom he had ever known. Now he wanted to share it with others.

Heilprin was shocked to learn that slavery advocates used Rabbi Raphall's sermon as ammunition when they defended their views. The New York journalist feared that because the rabbi based his views on Jewish law many people would believe that he expressed the opinions of all American Jews. This sermon, Heilprin wrote, "may induce many people to believe that the God of the Jews was or is a God of slavery."

GUERRILLA FIGHTS IN KANSAS

Heilprin must have rejoiced to learn of the Jews who stood with that splendid rebel, John Brown. Kansas had become a battleground for the two forces, equally lawless, which battled over the question whether the Territory should enter the Union as a free or a slave state. As in every war, declared or unde-clared, there were many outrages on either side. The pro-slavery men had treated their opponents brutally and seemed on the point of driving them out of Kansas.

But in the spring of 1858 John Brown led his party of eight guerrilla fighters in an attack on Pottawatomie. This border skirmish in which five pro-slavery men were slaughtered seemed at first to be of little importance; but to all thoughtful citizens, North and South, it pointed out with terrible clearness that the question of slavery had passed the point of debates in the Senate and might have to be settled on a nation-wide battlefield.

Of the eight men who fought under the grizzled, radical leader, John Brown, three were Jews. The best known among them was August Bondi with his typical history of a tireless fight for freedom. When a fifteen-year-old student in Vienna, he left his books and joined the ranks in the Austrian Revolution of 1848. When the Revolution failed, young Bondi and his family were fortunate enough to escape to the United States.

He seems never to have forgotten the brutal treatment of slaves which he witnessed in the South shortly after his arrival in this country. He settled in St. Louis where he tried many ways of earning his bread as drygoods clerk, printer's apprentice and school teacher. One day he read a newspaper appeal "to rush to Kansas and save it from the curse of slavery."

Bondi responded to this call as readily as he later answered President Lincoln's demand for volunteers to save the Union. He may have hesitated to enlist because he felt his wife and child needed his support. But his mother, Bondi tells us in his autobiography, promised to take care of them during his absence. He adds proudly: "My mother said that as a *Jehudi* I had a duty to perform, to defend the institutions which gave equal rights to all beliefs." He served as First Sergeant in the Kansas Volunteer Cavalry until the last year of the war when his dangerous wounds brought him his discharge.

The veteran returned to Kansas to hold several public offices. He loved to tell stories of his first battles on the barricades of Vienna; he boasted that he had once served under John Brown of whom the Union soldiers sang as they marched. Still a fighter at seventy years, he wrote what might have been the epitaph of the men of '48:

"I do not regret a single step in my long life to further the realization of my devout wishes that tyranny and despotism may perish, and bigotry and fanaticism may be wiped from the face of the earth."

HOW TWO RABBIS FOUGHT THE WAR

When the long feared war began in 1861 every Jew, North and South, realized how hopeless it was to try to remain neutral. Although certain church bodies like the Methodist and the Baptist groups split on the question of slavery, no actual cleavage occurred in the synagogue. Of course Jews everywhere all over the United States had to take a definite stand. How necessary it was to do this appears in the stories

Rabbi David Einhorn

of two American rabbis of Civil War days.

Rabbi David Einhorn hated slavery and denounced it both from his Baltimore pulpit and in the Jewish paper he edited. Maryland was a border state, strongly Southern in its sympathies. Baltimore was not a city where it was safe to preach or write against slavery. Rabbi Einhorn's friends urged him for the sake of his own safety to be silent; his enemies abused and threatened him. But the rabbi continued to defend what he considered the truth.

By the middle of April during the first days of the war there was rioting in the Baltimore streets between the citizens who had remained loyal to the Union and those who favored the Confederate cause. Soldiers came to the rabbi with a list of abolitionists the Southern sympathizers had doomed to die. David Einhorn saw his name among those the rioters had marked for death. His friends insisted that he must leave the city at once. He quietly refused.

To protect the rabbi and his family, a group of youths from his own congregation armed and volunteered to protect him. The rioting continued with its burning of homes and often murderous attacks on anyone accused of supporting the Union cause. Rabbi Einhorn feared for the lives of his young friends who stood guard before his door. They would be the first to suffer, the rabbi knew, should the mob attack his home. And if the rioters once crashed their frenzied way into the house what would become of his wife and children? A man has the right to choose his own death but how dare he sacrifice others for his cause?

The madness in the streets of Baltimore continued to mount in fury. After four days of suspense and horror Rabbi Einhorn admitted that he must take his family to safety. He promised to return to his congregation as soon as there was peace in the city.

Before a month had passed the congregation's Board of Trustees, who did not seem to share their rabbi's courage, wrote him that his pulpit would not be restored to him unless he promised not to write or speak against slavery. But Rabbi David Einhorn, a fighter from his youth, refused to surrender. He did not return to Baltimore.

158

A brother rabbi who was as devoted to the Confederacy as David Einhorn had shown himself to the Union was James K. Gutheim. Unlike Rabbi Einhorn he felt it was wrong to speak on political subjects from the pulpit. This attitude should have kept him out of trouble, but who is safe during a war?

When the Union forces took over New Orleans in 1863 the city was placed under military control. Every citizen was ordered to take an oath of allegiance to the United States; those who refused were sent to the states still under the control of the Confederacy. James K. Gutheim was then serving as the rabbi of the city's synagogue. He was asked to take the oath of allegiance and refused.

For he was loyal to the Confederacy and too honorable to perjure himself with a false oath. He was forced to give up his position and his home in the city which he loved. While the war lasted Rabbi Gutheim and his family remained in exile in Montgomery, Alabama.

"THE BRAINS OF THE CONFEDERACY"

One of the most prominent Jews in the South in 1861 was a man who had shed his loyalty to Judaism as easily as he changed his name Levy to the more acceptable Yulee. David Yulee was Senator from Florida; his allegiance to the Con-

federacy forced him to resign from the Senate. Since his Jewish origin was well known, anti-Semites throughout the Union never failed to brand him as a *Jewish* traitor.

The far more efficient Senator from Louisiana, Judah P. Benjamin, was a man born to make enemies. Northerners might couple his name with Yulee's and denounce him as Jew and traitor. But in the Confederacy itself he was even more heartily hated. His few friends might admire him for his truly Southern hospitality, his princely generosity, his undoubted talents. But his many enemies envied him not only for his success as a lawyer and statesman; they sneered that he was a "typical Jew" in appearance, in his ostentatious display and his shrewdness.

Representing the deep South in the United States Senate before the war, Judah P. Benjamin stood foremost among the defenders of slavery. After one of his addresses, Benjamin F. Wade, the "free-soil Senator" from Ohio attempted to answer him. But instead of beginning his reply with counter arguments, he sneered: "I have listened with intense interest as I always do to the eloquent speech of my friend, the Senator from Louisiana—an Israelite with Egyptian principles."

Reminding Mr. Benjamin that he was a descendant of Hebrew slaves who had suffered from Egyptian cruelty was a most effective way of emphasizing that the Senator was not only pro-slavery but Jewish. As Judah P. Benjamin was anything but a loyal Jew, it seems a pity that many of his co-religionists suffered for his failings.

And he had many! At least the citizens of the Confederate States found much to criticize in the able statesmen who had always defended their institutions.

When Jefferson Davis, President of the Confederacy, first appointed Mr. Benjamin a member of his cabinet, some of his political enemies called him a "foreigner." This may have been due to his Jewish origin or to the fact that he was born in the British West Indies. But, urged his defenders, he came to this country at an early age, was brought up in Charleston and educated at Yale!

President Davis, however, sadly needed the legal knowledge and keen intelligence which won for Benjamin the title, "the Brains of the Confederacy." The former Senator successively held three posts in the cabinet: Attorney-General, Secretary of War and Secretary of State.

He managed to keep this most important office until the fall of the Confederacy. Although he was never personally attracted to Mr. Benjamin, President Davis was always keenly aware of his merits. He refused to heed the complaint of a Richmond writer that it was blasphemous for a Jew to hold such a high office and that the prayers of the Confederacy would have more effect if Benjamin were dropped from the cabinet. Nor was Mr. Davis too much concerned when a citizen of North Carolina raved that "all the distresses of the people were owing to a Nero-like despotism, originating in the brain of Benjamin the Jew."

For four weary years the war dragged on. The Confederacy, at first so confident of victory, began to feel not only the heaviness of defeat but the pinch of hunger. Not only the "poor whites" but the proud first families of the South began to complain of their privations. In Richmond, the capital, there was much talk of those who although they pretended to serve the cause "cornered the market" and sold at outrageous prices the food they had accumulated. The citizens of Richmond were heard to complain that even while their children went hungry to bed every night, Mrs. Jefferson Davis served rich cakes at her afternoon teas and invited a chosen few to her lavish dinners.

Of course, Judah P. Benjamin came in for a goodly share of such criticism. The housing situation in the overcrowded capital was growing more desperate every day. Yet Mr. Benjamin, a wealthy brother-in-law and several Congressmen occupied a mansion which many considered far too large for their needs. The Secretary of War had long lived in Louisiana where he had acquired a taste for rich and bountiful foods and rare wines. Perhaps the stories of his war-time banquets are grossly exaggerated. But the hungry citizens of Richmond had grown irritable and sullen; they were more than ready to listen to any rumor.

But even more serious were the charges leveled against Benjamin as Secretary of War. The Southern armies after their first brilliant victories began to falter and even to retreat; their military failures, which filled the streets with black-robed women, were blamed on Judah P. Benjamin. He was denounced as President Davis' "evil genius." A general who was defeated at Roanoke Island charged he had not been given proper support by the Secretary of War. The Confederate Congress censured Benjamin for his failure to send a sufficient quantity of guns and ammunition; the Secretary of War did not try to defend himself. His defense, which he withheld in order not to lower public morale, would have been very simple: he had had no supplies to send.

After that it was impossible to allow Mr. Benjamin to remain the head of the War Department. But President Davis was grateful and assigned him to the post of Secretary of State. What the Confederacy needed most at that moment was the recognition of a strong foreign power like England. Her mill owners sadly needed Southern cotton and were willing to ignore their government's anti-slavery sympathies. Then in 1863 spectacular Northern victories at Vicksburg and Gettysburg completely crushed any hopes the Confederacy might have entertained of recognition by England. Few nations care to favor a losing cause and from that fatal month of July the Confederacy was doomed to slow but certain defeat.

Judah P. Benjamin, who had known much undeserved criticism and ingratitude from the South, remained loyal to her to the end. Word from General Robert E. Lee that he would not be able to defend Richmond reached the doomed capital. Both President Davis and his Secretary of State attempted to flee from the Union troops.

Benjamin was fortunate enough to escape to England where he was granted British citizenship and resumed his law practise. As always he was highly successful in his profession. After his stormy adventure in the United States, he again knew wealth and social prestige. He continued to practise law for sixteen years; then he retired to spend his last days playing chess in Paris, where he died in his seventy-third year.

ABRAHAM LINCOLN, FRIEND OF THE JEWS—AND ALL MANKIND

We Jews in our love for Abraham Lincoln sometimes over-emphasize his friendliness for our people. Until he reached manhood it is unlikely that he had ever met a single Jew outside the pages of the family Bible. The backwoods boy had educated himself almost entirely from this one Book. As Jews we may be proud that our Scriptures did much to influence the self-taught lawyer's prose style and mold his character.

Anyone who has studied the personal history of this great-hearted man must realize that Abraham Lincoln's warm friend-liness embraced Negro and white, Jew and Christian, alien and native-born. He singled out no particular group; as he himself said, when questioned on the rights of certain German immigrants: "I have some little notoriety for commiserating the oppressed condition of the Negro and I should be strangely inconsistent if I should favor any project for curtailing the existing rights of white men, even though born in different lands and speaking different languages from myself."

In 1860 Chicago's convention hall, the Wigwam, seemed to rock with the shouts of the delegates who had just nominated Abraham Lincoln for president. A number of Jews actively supported the lawyer from Springfield. One of Lincoln's staunchest Jewish friends was Abraham Jonas, a Quincy attorney and a member of the state legislature. He had already done much to bring Lincoln before the public in Illinois; now he spoke and organized for his friend in the presidential campaign.

President Lincoln never forgot a favor. There is no record of Abraham Jonas asking for a reward for his aid, but when a mutual friend reminded Mr. Lincoln that his former supporter "should be remembered in connection with the Post Office at Quincy," the president quickly appointed him to that office.

This was shortly after President Lincoln's inauguration.

But in the last year of the war a far more urgent appeal came to Washington. The same mutual friend informed Mr. Lincoln that four of Abraham Jonas' sons were fighting on the Confederate side. One of them, Charles, had been captured and was now held as a prisoner of war. Mr. Jonas lay dying, the friend continued, and Mrs. Jonas wondered whether it would be possible for the boy to be sent home long enough to bid his father farewell.

The President issued the required parole; Charles returned to Quincy on the day his father died. Shortly afterward President Lincoln appointed Mr. Jonas' widow to serve his unexpired term in the Post Office at Quincy.

A happier story tells how Abraham Kohn, Chicago's city clerk, celebrated Abraham Lincoln's election to the presidency. The two had met a number of times and had discussed both politics and the Bible. Mr. Kohn, like President Lincoln, seems not only to have known the Scriptures very well but to have possessed the knack of using just the right quotation at the right time. As a parting gift for the President-elect, the Chicago Jew painted an American flag; across it he lettered the heart-lifting words of Moses to his general, Joshua: "Be strong and of good courage; be not afraid, neither be thou dismayed; for the Lord thy God is with thee whithersoever thou goest."

According to John Hay, one of the presidential secretaries, Lincoln carried this picture to the White House. During the dark days that followed his election, when the Union cause seemed lost, did the gaunt, sad-faced man, troubled with many cares, ever recall those singing words and find new courage to return to the battle?

JEWISH SOLDIERS, NORTH AND SOUTH

When Lincoln issued his call for volunteers, the Jews were honorably represented in the ranks who marched to their training camps and loudly sang, "We are coming, Father Abraham." At the same time a goodly number of the young Jews of the South gathered under the Stars and Bars. It is rather difficult to estimate just how many Jews served in the Northern and Southern armies. Many soldiers were not listed by their religion, which can only be guessed by considering distinctively Jewish names; a number of the states did not have complete records. But it has been estimated that over 6,000 Jews fought for the Union while 1,200 to 1,500 served in the Confederate forces.

As in every other war in our Republic's history, certain Jews in both armies rose high in the service; others in the ranks by heroic sacrifices conferred honor upon their people. From the Hungarian immigrant, Brigadier General Frederick Knefler, who shared Sherman's march through Georgia, to twenty-one-year-old Marx E. Cohen of Charleston, who died on the battlefield that his comrades might live, Jewish soldiers fought bravely and well.

Both North and South, the Jews behind the lines did their part. In every city Jewish women helped to organize sanitary fairs and raise money to purchase comforts for the military; they rolled bandages and visited the sick and wounded who filled the hospitals. During the first year of the war our old friend Miss Rebecca Gratz reminded the members of her Hebrew Benevolent Society that soldiers' families in Philadelphia must be provided for.

THE FIRST JEWISH CHAPLAINS IN THE UNITED STATES ARMY

Although Jews never demanded any exceptional treatment as a group, they insisted that there should be no discrimination against them. Through excellent leadership and prompt action they gained two very worth while victories for themselves— and for American democracy as well.

In former wars of these United States, from the Revolution down to the Mexican War, Christian chaplains of various denominations had been appointed by our government to serve with the armed forces.

In 1861 the Jews of the Confederacy realized that because

they were scattered through so many regiments no single group was large enough to ask that a rabbi be appointed to care for its religious needs. Of course, whenever possible, rabbis tried to help Jewish boys in the service to observe their religion.

Every year as the High Holy Days approached, Rabbi M. J. Michelbacher of Richmond requested that the Jewish men in the Virginia area be given furloughs to attend services. Every year General Robert E. Lee or one of his officers would answer that because of the military situation, it was impossible to spare so many men from duty at a given time.

But although he was always disappointed, Rabbi Michelbacher rejoiced over the sympathy and understanding in the Commander in Chief's letters. For he knew, as every one of Lee's countless admirers knew, that the general was a God-faring man, who because he respected his own religion respected the religion of others. To quote from one of the letters Robert E. Lee wrote the rabbi during the first year of the war:

"I feel assured that neither you nor any member of the Jewish congregation would wish to jeopardize a cause you have so much at heart by the withdrawal even for a season of a portion of its defenders. . . . Should any be deprived of the opportunity of offering up their prayers according to the rites of their Church (I trust) their penitence may nevertheless be accepted by the Most High and their petitions answered."

It was different in the Union forces. In several of the Eastern states so many Jews were on the army rolls that their number justified the appointment of Jewish chaplains. It was not only because a sick or dying soldier longed for a rabbi to comfort him. Jews felt that the existing law that only Christian clergymen might serve as military chaplains was discriminatory. As a result of strong Jewish protests Congress amended the law and President Lincoln appointed two rabbis as hospital chaplains. Rabbi Ferdinand L. Sarner was elected chaplain by the officers of the 54th New York infantry; his services carried him to the front; he was wounded at Gettysburg.

AN INSULT TO EVERY JEW!

This matter of discrimination concerning army chaplains was serious enough. But in the same year the Jews of the North faced a much more serious problem.

As General Ulysses S. Grant advanced into enemy territory, there was an increase of violations of the blockade which the Union had imposed on the South. Some traders followed the Northern forces on pretense of supplying the soldiers' wants; they were actually smugglers who managed to bring desperately needed medicine, clothing and the like into the Confederate states. There were also other criminal practises connected with the sale of cotton and carrying Union money into the South.

To put a stop to this illegal traffic Army Headquarters issued Order No. 11. After all these years it is still hard for a Jew to read it calmly:

"The Jews, as a class violating every regulation of trade established by the Treasury Department and also department orders, are hereby expelled from the department within twenty-four hours from the receipt of this order.

"Post commanders will see that all of this class of people be furnished passes and required to leave, and any one returning after such notification will be arrested and held in confinement until an opportunity occurs of sending them as prisoners, unless furnished with permit from headquarters.

"No passes will be given these people to visit headquarters for the purpose of making personal application for trade permits."

The friends of General Grant claimed later that although this order came from Grant's office, it had been issued without his knowledge. Whether General Grant was guilty or not of making these sweeping and insulting charges was beside the question in 1861. The Jews, who felt that they had done all in their power to aid the Union, now found themselves set apart and disgraced in the eyes of their fellow-citizens.

But why were Jews mentioned in this Order as the only offenders?

171

The men who followed the army as traders were drawn from nearly every group. No one could deny that some of the criminals mentioned were Jews. It is possible that some of the recent immigrants among the traders were conspicuous not only because of their speech but their appearance.

Throughout the Union the Jews cried that it was unjust to besmirch the good name of an entire people because of the crime of a few. They were naturally concerned with the rough treatment accorded certain Jewish traders; one man was not given enough time even to dispose of his horse and buggy before he was expelled from the area; the Order made it impossible for any Jew, no matter how honorable his business record, to secure a trading permit. But most outrageous of all was the implication that Jews *as a class* were dishonest business men and disloyal to the Union.

KENTUCKY SENDS A CHAMPION TO WASHINGTON

The challenge was taken up promptly by a young business man of Paducah, Kentucky. Cesar J. Kaskel up to this time had known the uneventful life of a merchant in the easy-going little border town. But now he prepared to fight—and to fight hard!—for the good name of his people and the honor of

Democracy.

Mr. Kaskel was also personally concerned; he was one of a small group of Jewish merchants living in Paducah who now faced financial ruin and even exile. During the early days of the war Grant's forces had occupied the town, which was openly sympathetic to the Confederacy and had been placed under military regulations. So Paducah was now considered as part of the "department" to be affected. The authorities were forced to obey orders from Headquarters; they notified the Jewish merchants and their families to leave within twenty-four hours.

Now begins one of the most shameful episodes in American Jewish history. Not one of the thirty Jews who were forced to leave Paducah at this time had ever been engaged in trade with the army; they could not possibly be classed as offenders. A number of these Kentucky merchants had openly supported the Union; two had served in its armies. Non-Jews were indignant when they heard of a baby said to have been abandoned by the frantic family; it was remembered just before the mother reached the river boats which were to carry the refugees into exile. Two women were so ill that the officials allowed them to remain behind in the care of kindly neighbors.

Cesar Kaskel and several other Paducah Jews had already written to President Lincoln. They declared that the carrying out of Order No. 11 "would be the grossest violation of the Constitution and our rights as citizens under it." It is unlikely that in the stress and excitement of wartime this message ever reached the President, for there was no answer. Mr. Kaskel decided he would see what could be accomplished by a personal visit to the White House.

Cesar Kaskel was not a romantic figure like Paul Revere calling his countrymen to arms; instead of springing on a snorting, galloping horse he took passage on one of the low white boats on the Ohio River. As the vessel moved all too slowly from Paducah to Cincinnati, the impatient champion wrote letters and telegrams "to spread the alarm" to Jewish community leaders and the editors of the Jewish newspapers. He urged every Jew in the North to protest to Washington. Before Kaskel reached the capital the President's desk was piled high with messages from every part of the Union, all appealing to the Chief Executive for justice.

In Cincinnati Mr. Kaskel held a hasty conference with Rabbi Isaac M. Wise and other leaders of the Jewish community; he described what had happened in Paducah and several other neighboring towns; he urged immediate action. In Washington at last, he asked a friend of Rabbi Wise, Congressman Gurley, to accompany him to the White House.

Abraham Lincoln, almost crushed beneath the cares of a wartime President, appeared to know very little concerning the hateful order. He listened attentively to Kaskel's carefully prepared brief. Then the worn-faced man adjusted his spectacles to glance over the letters which Mr. Kaskel had brought from leading citizens and the military authorities. These proved that the Jews who had suffered expulsion had done nothing to warrant the severity of Grant's order.

Several of Abraham Lincoln's more pompous Cabinet members liked to complain that whenever they brought up very serious matters for discussion the President delayed business by telling an irrelevant joke or story. Now when he heard of the exodus of the Kentucky Jews, he asked with a half-smile:

"And so the Children of Israel were driven from the happy land of Canaan?"

Mr. Kaskel's answer suggests that he was not only as quick to plunge into action as Paul Revere but resembled another early patriot, Benjamin Franklin, in his ready wit.

"Yes," he replied, "and that is why we have come unto Father Abraham's bosom asking protection."

"And this protection they shall have at once," promised the President.

Turning to his desk, he hastily penned a note to the army's General-in-Chief and directed him immediately to cancel Order 11. He held out a huge work-weathered hand to Kaskel and wished him a safe journey back to Paducah.

A few days later several rabbis and a number of prominent laymen from Cincinnati, Louisville and Baltimore reached Washington. Without taking time even to tidy their travel-stained clothes, the delegation hastened to the White House to thank President Lincoln. He emphatically told his visitors that "to condemn a class is to wrong the good with the bad", and added: "I do not like to hear a class or nationality condemned on account of a few sinners."

In spite of its short life Order No. 11 was of the greatest importance to American Jews. Their speedy and widespread response gave strong evidence of the growing pride and unity among our people. While their firm demand for justice did much to convince the lawmakers of our nation that the Jews of the United States would never submit to the indignity of second-class citizenship.

DEATH OF A PROPHET

Mr. Lincoln's swift recognition of Jewish rights both in the matter of army chaplains and Order No. 11 did much to increase the love and respect the Jews of the Union felt for their President. But no one realized how strong that love had grown until a Sabbath morning in early April when heart-sick telegraphers tapped their unhappy message to every corner of the land.

Jews on their way to synagogue learned that the President, brought low by an assassin's bullet, had died early that morning. Some rabbis wept and were unable to address their grief-stricken congregations. Others paid the first public tribute to the martyred man, for memorial services were not held in the churches until the following Sunday.

Many eloquent sermons have been preserved for us in the memorial volume, *Abraham Lincoln, the Tribute of the Synagogue* by Emanuel Hertz. It is hard to select the one which best expresses the spirit of this friend to the Jews and to all humanity. But of the many which I have read, I like best the sermon delivered by Rabbi Samuel Adler of Temple Emanu El in New York. He compares the dead President to Moses, for both served their people faithfully, yet were forced to leave their work unfinished:

"How terrible that Abraham Lincoln, having performed a portion of his duty, should be taken away by the hand of destiny before he completed it. This sad event was the will of God, and we must bear it calmly, as if a prophet had died."

part three

WE PAY OUR
DEBT TO AMERICA

A LULL IN IMMIGRATION

For four hard years Jews in the Union and the Confederacy had found it difficult to look after their own interests. In wartime a community seldom builds a church or schoolhouse; cultural and social activities are neglected.

During this period there had been very little Jewish immigration into the United States, for who wants to face conditions in a country torn by war? We have seen that hardships in Germany and disappointment over the failure of the Revolution drove thousands of Europeans to our shores. But even after the Civil War was over Jewish immigration continued to dwindle. We may trace this decline to two causes: since financial conditions had greatly improved in Germany, there was less urge to emigrate and a more liberal government had by slow degrees granted the German Jews the rights of citizenship.

The German Jews who had become American citizens were now firmly rooted in this country. Although many of them still enjoyed their German Singing Societies, they nearly all read English newspapers and became interested in American politics. Many of them had come to the United States bitterly poor; they had been forced to borrow enough to pay for the odds and ends of merchandise which they carried on their backs from farmhouse to farmhouse and from village to village.

These peddlers, hardworking and thrifty, prospered. Soon many of them had saved enough to buy a horse and wagon; another year or two, maybe three or four, and they were able to set up a little store in a little town. Often the store and the town grew up together. In Columbus, Ohio, we find F & R Lazarus, the largest department store in the state, with several flourishing branches. It is a family legend that the founder of the firm in 1851 began business in his little wooden shop by exchanging a few staples with an Indian chief for a buffalo hide.

Our Jewish merchant often remained in the town to become in every sense a member of the community. If there were no Jewish lodges, he might join the Masons. Even when more Jewish families arrived there were still not enough women to form a Sisterhood; but our merchant's wife found a welcome in the Ladies' Aid Society of one of the local churches. She always baked cakes for their church suppers; her husband never failed to give a liberal donation when the Presbyterian Church needed a new carpet or the Catholic Parochial School a new bell. Since this handful of Jews had no religious school of its own, some of the parents allowed their children to attend Sunday School with their playmates.

In some cases these small town Jews were absorbed by the

majority group and were lost to Judaism. But often, if a sufficient number of Jewish families joined them, some devoted
soul would organize services at least for the fall Holy Days.
Or a mother would arrange to teach a weekly class in her
home that the handful of Jewish children would not grow up
without any knowledge of their religion. As the Jewish community grew, it repeated the progress of the Sephardim of
colonial days. The loosely organized congregation which had
worshiped in a store loft began to talk of hiring a rabbi and
building a synagogue.

The Original Lazarus Store

The Present Lazarus Store

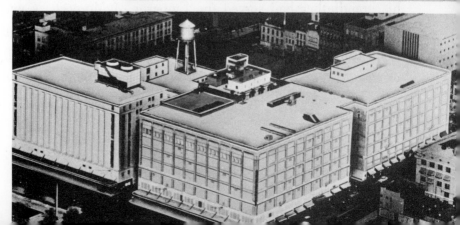

At first the German congregations were all Orthodox; but later many followed the teachings of Reform Judaism. This movement, which began in Germany, took a long time to establish itself firmly in the United States. But as early as 1824 a number of the younger members of the old Congregation Beth Elohim of Charleston suggested certain changes in the ritual. They not only wanted the traditional service to be shortened, but argued that some of the prayers should be read in English. And what about an English sermon every week?

The trustees of the Charleston congregation refused to consider such radical changes; some of the younger members, led by Isaac Harby, withdrew to establish the "Reformed Society of Israelites."

Isaac Harby reminds us in several ways of our dashing friend, Mordecai Noah; he, too, was a successful writer, with Noah's generous nature and pioneering spirit. Although Harby never furthered any scheme half so picturesque as Noah's City of Ararat, he could at least boast more romantic ancestors, for his grandfather had served the Emperor of Morocco as one of the royal jewelers. Although Mr. Harby studied law, he never cared to practise it. For a time he conducted a successful private school; but his real interest was in writing; soon we find him following Mr. Noah as a playwright and journalist. Today Isaac Harby's plays are forgotten along with the political articles which were written for the Charleston papers he edited. But the author's vigorous personality, his genius for friendship still appeal to those who know the story of his life.

Mr. Harby was a radical not only in politics but in religion. He believed whole-heartedly in the ideas of Reform Judaism. But not even he could save the Reformed Society of Israelites. Its members although sincere and enthusiastic did not represent the wealthier, "solid" members of the Jewish community. Their first president, Mr. Harby, not only lacked rabbinical training but was often obliged to give all of his time to his political and literary interests. After eight years the Society disbanded. But later a number of the changes these pioneers had advocated were adopted by the older and more Orthodox congregation.

ORTHODOX AND REFORM

Just what is meant by the terms Orthodox and Reform? You who read this are likely to belong to either one or to the third group usually described as Conservative. Personally, we do not like the term, Reform Judaism, since it seems to suggest that its founders discovered many faults in Orthodoxy;

that the Jews who practise it feel themselves superior to other groups. Many of us prefer the friendlier title, Liberal Judaism, and use the original name only because it is more familiar.

Now just what changes did the "Reformers," first in Germany and later in the United States, wish to bring about in the synagogue ritual and Jewish customs?

In both countries certain leaders felt the need for a more modern way of worship. They declared that in their long, long history the Jewish people had abandoned many ancient customs and adopted the new ones. They insisted that if the Jews wished to enjoy the rights of citizens they must act more like their Christian neighbors both in the synagogue and in their homes. This did not mean that any Jewish leader, no matter how eager he was for change, advocated dropping fundamental Jewish beliefs such as the immortality of the soul or the oneness of God.

But those who hoped to modernize the synagogue wished to introduce such changes as the family pew where women might sit with their fathers or husbands, instead of being relegated to the traditional gallery. They demanded an organ and a choir of men and women instead of one composed only of men with young boys to sing the soprano parts.

In the Reform service some prayers were shortened, others translated for the benefit of congregants who knew no Hebrew; certain passages which expressed the longing to return to Palestine were dropped altogether. It was argued that in a free country like the United States the Jews no longer felt themselves in exile. "America is our Palestine, Washington is our Jerusalem" might sound like a jest, but it was often uttered in painful earnest.

Other changes were suggested; they were rejected by the Orthodox group since the truly Orthodox Jew does not welcome change. He bases his way of life both in the synagogue and in his home on the *Shulchan Aruch,* a codification of laws prepared in Palestine in 1572.

Many of the early Reform rabbis were in favor of keeping any Jewish law which they considered meaningful or for the preservation of the Jewish people. Not one of them dreamed of abolishing the Jewish rest day. But because so many Jewish business men in America seemed unable to attend services on Saturday morning, it was decided to have the principal Sabbath service on Friday night. Again, although many of these Reform leaders found no harm in eating forbidden food in restaurants or at the tables of their Christian friends, they were careful to maintain a kosher kitchen in their own homes.

One of these leaders who really loved the old Jewish customs, but advocated dropping those which he believed were obsolete, was Rabbi Isaac M. Wise. We have chosen him to represent the Reform group in the United States. When he came to America Reform was a growing movement, but sorely needed a man with his genius for organization.

His was a long life filled with work and adventure. As he once said of himself: "I have written much, worked much and been more lauded and abused than any other man of my age." He might have added that the extravagant praise he received from his friends did not make him overbearing and conceited; that his enemies' abuse failed to embitter his warm, cheerful nature. In his open-handed charity he often gave the very coat from his back when a beggar stopped him on the street, and returned home, a rather undignified figure in his shirt sleeves. But he showed an even greater generosity when his opponents misunderstood his motives and refused to listen to his explanations.

But do not picture Isaac M. Wise as a gentle saint. For all his friendliness he was a fighter who seemed to thrive on the excitement of the battle as well as the cause he fought for. As a young man he refused to submit to anti-Jewish laws in his native Bohemia, then under the control of the tyrannical

Austro-Hungarian Empire. He tells us in his autobiography how he learned enough English to study some American newspapers which contained the debates on the Federal Constitution of 1787. He grew so excited that he felt he was already a naturalized American citizen. He believed that it was this experience which made him resolve to emigrate to the strange, distant country with freedom and opportunity for all her children.

As a young child he had studied Hebrew with his father, the teacher of the local Jewish school. When Wise left home for more advanced courses in the Yeshiva, he depended on the kindness of families who followed the old Jewish custom of regularly inviting Yeshiva students to share their meals. Later he supported himself by giving lessons to young children. He also managed to receive a good secular education, which included a year of study at the University of Vienna.

While Wise served his apprenticeship as the rabbi of a small town he was greatly influenced by the ideas of some of the German leaders of the new Reform movement. He grew more and more dissatisfied with his congregation who were not yet ready for the changes he wished to introduce; he hated more and more the restrictions the government placed upon his people. It was a daring thing for a professional man of twenty-seven with a wife and child to pull up roots and start life all over again in a new country. And there were the usual governmental restrictions about granting him a passport. As always, difficulties spurred him on. In 1846 the young rabbi came to America.

Here his first pulpit was in Albany, New York. Although the congregation was made up of German immigrants, Rabbi Wise insisted upon preaching in English. In his sermons and in the articles he soon began to write for America's first Jewish paper, the "Occident," the rabbi fearlessly defended Reform Judaism. The suggestions he made for changes which would make it easier for Jews to fit into American life would be acceptable to Conservative congregations today. But many of the Albany Jews considered Isaac M. Wise far too radical to be their rabbi.

The storm of criticism and accusations finally broke during a Rosh Hashonah service. When Rabbi Wise attempted to take the Torah from the Ark, the president of the congregation attacked him and knocked him down. There were enough members who sympathized with the rabbi and his ideas to form another congregation under his leadership. But how could a religious leader be happy in a city where half the Jewish community remained violently opposed to him and his teaching? Perhaps, he thought, there will be a better chance to establish a stronger and a freer Judaism in the newly settled West.

So in 1854 Isaac M. Wise welcomed the call to serve Bene Yeshurun Congregation of Cincinnati. He remained its rabbi until his death.

The Ohio city, which in years to come was to be known as the Cradle of Reform Judaism in America, had welcomed its first Jew in 1817. Jonathan Jonas, brother of President Lincoln's early friend, was an English Jew. At first Jewish settlers in Cincinnati were almost exclusively English; but by 1830 Jewish immigrants from Germany began to outnumber them. These German Jews warmly welcomed the then radical changes Rabbi Wise suggested; they stood behind him in his many important efforts to build and strengthen Reform Judaism.

The rabbi tells us that during his first years in America he worked eighteen hours a day. This is hard to believe; when we review the record of his achievements, we wonder how anyone could accomplish half so much even if his strength had permitted him to work twenty-four hours.

Of course, his first duty was to his congregation which he served faithfully for forty-six years. The mere list of the books and articles he wrote would cover many pages. He modernized and translated the Prayer Book; he wrote text books for Jewish children and scholarly papers to help non-Jews understand Jewish theology. Because he could not find suitable stories of Jewish life for his paper "Deborah," he actually wrote a number of historical novels, grinding out a chapter every week. Often he was too rushed to outline his contribution or even to check it for errors before it was snatched up by the printer. Once, he confessed later, he forgot the name of his heroine and hastily gave her a new one. This left Rabbi Wise's hero with two sweethearts! It was a shocking situation which the flustered author corrected the following week by dooming one of the girls to die in a fire in the Frankfort ghetto.

Isaac M. Wise and "The Israelite"

"Deborah" was written in German; it became the "Ladies Home Journal" of Jewish women who still preferred literature in their native language. Their number dwindled; the next generation of Jewesses attended public school and turned to the English story papers for their romances. But Dr. Wise's other journalistic brain-child was the 'American Israelite'. The two papers were published by Bloch & Co. founded in Cincinnati in 1854 by Isaac M. Wise and Edward Bloch. The firm, now Bloch Publishing Company in New York, observed in 1954 its one hundredth anniversary.

After the close of the Civil War, with all of the Reform Jews of the country united behind him, the rabbi began the most important work of his life—the building of needed institutions and organizations.

The period which began in 1865 and ended in 1880 was the time when the German Jews made their greatest contributions to Jewish life in America. They had acquired considerable wealth; Rabbi Wise and other leaders had stirred their interests. These one-time immigrants had brought from their Fatherland their love of organization whether it meant forming a lodge or building an orphanage or planning a Young Men's Hebrew Association in New York City.

They listened with enthusiasm as Rabbi Wise on his many speaking tours through the country outlined his plans. They agreed that if Reform Judaism were to flourish, the new congregation springing up all over the land must be united. So now in 1873 a number joined forces in the Union of American Hebrew Congregations.

With the support of this body Rabbi Wise, who recognized how desperately Reform Judaism needed American-trained rabbis, opened his school. He tells us how the Hebrew Union College began in the basement of a Cincinnati synagogue with one teacher and "the exalted president" to instruct fourteen

193

noisy boys of high school age. "The president and the faculty alternately took each group. No one who failed to see the embryonic college can imagine how ridiculous was this little hole-in-the-wall of a school, in its none-too-bright cellar, carrying the pompous name of a college. Fortunately we did not have to be ashamed in front of visitors, for none came. Also, no book was stolen since each evening the whole library was locked up in a two-and-one-half foot box, not because of thieves but because of mice."

The four rabbis in the first graduation class became leaders in the Reform movement. Year after year the number of graduates grew; they left Cincinnati to occupy pulpits or to engage in various types of Jewish work not only in the United States but, as time passed, in Canada, in England, in Australia and South Africa, and at last in the land of Israel.

Even when he was a very old man Isaac M. Wise continued to serve the college as instructor and president. In 1950 the Hebrew Union College united with the Jewish Institute of Religion of New York City; under the joint names the two seminaries train rabbis and scholars and builders of Reform Judaism.

In speaking of the growth of the synagogue in this country we have used such terms as Reform (or Liberal), Conservative and Orthodox. In our day these are the three largest and most important branches of Judaism. At this time we will not discuss the beginnings of Conservative Judaism in the United

States as that movement did not become really important in America until the first years of the twentieth century.

We have already given what we believe is the chief difference between the Reform and the Orthodox point of view. During this period there were a number of learned and conscientious American leaders who defended Orthodoxy. Again we have not the space to name them all but will tell the story of just one Orthodox leader, Isaac Leeser.

THE SCHOLAR WHO GAVE AMERICAN JEWS THEIR BIBLE

Although Isaac Leeser was not yet twenty when he came to the United States, he had already received an excellent education in his native Germany and laid the foundations for outstanding Hebrew scholarship. He was soon called to serve the historic Mikveh Israel synagogue in Philadelphia. One of the most important of his many, many accomplishments was the founding of the "Occident." The leading Jewish writers contributed to this paper, which, until Rabbi Wise established the "Israelite," was the only Jewish paper published in the United States. Scanning this journal today is like reviewing the record of the American Jews through twenty-five of the most formative years of our history.

Isaac Leeser was a tireless writer. Although he was the greatest Jewish scholar in America at this period, he did not feel it was beneath his dignity to prepare a very simple text book for young children, which, by the way, he dedicated to the founder and superintendent of his Sunday School, Miss Rebecca Gratz. He prepared a Sephardic prayer book and made many translations from the Hebrew. Perhaps his greatest service to our people is his translation of our Bible from Hebrew into English.

Up to that time Jews without sufficient Hebrew to read the original Scriptures were forced to depend on the King James version. This translation by a group of English Biblical scholars has always been considered a literary masterpiece. But Jews found little pleasure in reading it, as the Christian translators scattered frequent references to the New Testament through their version of the Old. Isaac Leeser's work was not only acceptable to Jewish scholars; it was so readable that it became the standard translation among all Jewish readers for more than fifty years. Finally it was replaced by a translation which was the work of a commission of Reform, Conservative and Orthodox scholars.

Like Rabbi Wise, the Philadelphia leader recognized the need for American trained rabbis; but the Seminary he tried to establish was not a success. He was happier in his efforts which ranged from pioneer work to place Jewish farmers on American soil to his labors for many Jewish organizations which still flourish in Philadelphia. His influence was tremendous; it extended far beyond the boundaries of the Eastern states where he had unified and strengthened Orthodoxy.

Although today Isaac Leeser is regarded as the champion and preserver of Orthodox Judaism and the enemy of the Reformers, he himself objected to labels and desired to serve a united Jewry. Once he said: "For our part, strange as it may seem, we belong to no party. We commenced life with certain convictions, and have not swerved from them. If you wish to call this orthodoxy, you may do so."

A "BAND OF BROTHERS"

Although the synagogues of the Orthodox and the temples of the Reformed Jews still played a very important part in American Jewish life, the German Jews, as we have mentioned earlier, founded a number of other institutions.

One of the earliest and most important was the Bnai Brith. In 1843 twelve young Jewish immigrants met in a restaurant in New York City to form a society. Their order was modeled largely on certain non-Jewish groups which met for social purposes, and provided insurance and sick benefits for their members. As these first members were all Germans it seemed right and proper to call themselves *Bundes Brueder* (Brothers of the Covenant). Later the name was changed into Bnai Brith, meaning in Hebrew, "Sons of the Covenant."

This organization grew rapidly, established lodges in other cities and in time became one of the most truly democratic groups in American Jewish life. Its membership came to include Jews of every type of religious belief, regardless of their birthplaces or backgrounds. Little by little the purpose of Bnai Brith broadened. When all of its first members were struggling to make a living, it seemed necessary to protect them with features like insurance and sick benefits. But as these new citizens grew prosperous enough to care for themselves and their families, this protection was dropped. Meanwhile the various lodges of the order began to establish large and important institutions like the Cleveland Orphan Asylum to care for all Jews who needed assistance.

Still later it took up what has proved its most constructive work, Jewish self defense. An effort was made to protect the rights of Jews in every country where they needed their American brethren to come to their defense. This effort was greatly aided by establishing Bnai Brith lodges in England, and Germany, in Turkey and Palestine.

In the United States it began the splendid work of the Anti-Defamation League. Before long every one of the many lodges throughout the United States had a committee to combat even the slightest injury to our reputation as good citizens. Happily this work of self defense again broadened to include co-operation with other minorities who suffer from discrimination.

At last came the Hillel Foundation movement by which Bnai Brith followed the example of many church groups and established centers for Jewish students on our college campuses.

Again we are sorry we cannot even list the many other fine Jewish organizations which began during this period. But we have spent too much time already on the period which extended from the end of the Civil War to the beginning of the Russian migration which is the next great adventure in our story.

THE THIRD WAVE OF IMMIGRATION—THE RUSSIAN

The third wave of Jewish immigration which began about 1880 is usually called "Russian" since about eighty-five percent of the Jews who arrived at that time came from the Russian Empire. This "wave" continued to rise steadily, until in 1924 when the gates of America were definitely closed against immigration and many unfortunates, Jews and non-Jews alike, knocked in vain upon the Golden Door.

CASTLE GARDEN

EMMA LAZARUS, THE POET OF HER PEOPLE

Who first thought of that happy phrase which has been used again and again by those who tell the story of Jewish adventures in America?

This seems a good place to relate her story, for the tale of the beginning of the great Russian migration and the life of Emma Lazarus should always be told together.

Emma Lazarus was born in New York City in 1849. Her family was wealthy, cultured and highly respected by Jew and Gentile alike; although she was taught to be proud of her descent from early Sephardic settlers in this country, the girl grew up with little knowledge of Judaism or pride in the Jewish people. She lived a secluded life, educated by private tutors and a close companion to her father, who supervised her reading and encouraged her first efforts to write poetry.

These early poems show how painfully unaware the girl was of the glories and tragedies of Israel. When she wrote of the Jewish synagogue at Newport, the lines are less Jewish in feeling than the more familiar verses penned by Longfellow. She was an excellent linguist; her early translations and adaptations of German legends won her the admiration and friendship of leading poets of her day, such as Ralph Waldo Emerson and William Morris, whom she later visited in his English home.

She continued to live in her sheltered corner filled with music and poetry and art until the news from overseas roused her from her pleasant dreaming. The Jews under the Czars had always been among the poorest of the poor, the most persecuted among the oppressed. It was hard to imagine how man's cruelty could cause them to suffer more; but now new sorrows crashed down upon the unfortunates.

First came the pogroms. These were not outbreaks against the Jews due to the anti-Semitism of their poor and ignorant neighbors. Whenever a revolt of the masses threatened, the autocratic Russian government attempted to divert the just anger of the people against the Czar and his officials. It was not difficult to convince the hungry and the hopeless that the Jews prevented them from making a comfortable living and constantly cheated and robbed honest, God-fearing Russians. The news of these massacres spread rapidly; Jews, even if they lived at some distance from the scene of the outrages, became panic stricken and tried to escape, while there was still time, to America.

In 1882 came the May Laws, so named because in that month the Russian Jews faced a new and terrible persecution. Many restrictive laws were passed; the most terrifying forced hundreds and hundreds of Jewish families out of the villages where they and their fathers before them had spent their lives. Now they were ordered to live in already overcrowded towns and cities, where they would have even less chance than before to make a decent living for their families.

The fires of new pogroms flared up through unhappy Russia. Death at the hands of an uncurbed mob or death by slow starvation? To the protests of these tortured thousands the Russian official hinted: "Nobody has put obstacles in the way of your emigration." The greatest flight in Jewish history since the Exodus of 1492 began. Always before they left for America the emigrants visited their cemeteries to bid farewell to those long beyond the fear of violence or exile. In many villages the dead were the only Jews who remained behind.

The uprooted migrants waited at Ward's Island in New York for relatives already in the United States to meet them. Women who represented various Jewish charities came to the ugly, cheerless building with words of welcome for the newcomers and—what was more readily understood—baskets of fruit and other strange dainties. Emma Lazarus, slight and frail in her modest bonnet and rich velvet cloak, longed to talk to the bearded grandfathers whose eyes were wells of tragic memories and unanswered prayers; but she did not know Yiddish and they shook their heads at her "book German." It was easier with the mothers; their worn, pinched faces broke into timid smiles when the American lady cooed to

202

their little ones in a universal language, or dangled a toy or a rosy apple before a frightened child.

The too protective Lazarus family worried about Emma's health. Surely, her visits to Ward's Island left her too fatigued. Her relatives would have been really alarmed could they have known how night after night the faces of the Russian immigrants haunted her and would not allow her to rest. She knew that if these unhappy souls had been willing to renounce their religion they might have lived in safety in Russia, that the intellectuals among them might have entered the professions and earned gold and honor for themselves. She asked herself again and again: What is this Judaism for which these people have been willing to face such a terrible martyrdom?

Emma Lazarus began to study the history and religion of her people. She thrilled at the heroism of the Maccabees and wrote "The Banner of the Jew," which is still recited in our religious schools. She read how a whole Jewish community in the fifteenth century faced the choice of conversion or death at the stake. For them there could be only one choice: men, women and even little children danced into the flames while they sang the praises of their God. Miss Lazarus put this glorious tragedy into a poetic play titled "The Dance to Death"; even more powerful is her poem, "Crowing of the Red Cock," in which she speaks of later martyrs in Russia.

Now instead of pale, pretty verses describing the woes of legendary heroes and heroines, her poetry tells of Jewish pioneers who labor to create another Promised Land. Before modern Zionism was born Emma Lazarus dreamed and wrote of the Return of the Exiles. She mastered Hebrew and translated the verses of an earlier and far greater poet than herself, Judah Halevi, lover of Zion. In this, her last productive period, she also wrote stirring articles in defense of her people, which appeared in the leading magazines of the day and were widely read and discussed.

Had she written nothing but the fourteen burning lines now inscribed at the base of the Statue of Liberty, this woman's name would always be remembered as a Jew and as an American.

She had seen with her own tear-filled eyes the feeble, bearded patriarchs, the burdened mothers and their children waiting in their temporary shelter and praying that at last they might enter the Land of Promise. So she came to think of "a mighty woman with a torch" which beamed a "world-wide welcome." The poet called the colossal statue "Mother of Exiles" and repeated her welcome:

"Keep, ancient lands, your storied pomp!" cries she,
With silent lips. "Give me your tired, your poor,
Your huddled masses yearning to breathe free,
The wretched refuse of your teeming shore.
Send these, the homeless, tempest-tost to me,—
I lift my lamp beside the golden door!"

Several years after Emma Lazarus wrote her immortal sonnet of welcome, not only to the Russian Jews but to all the oppressed of every land, she suffered a crushing loss in the death of her father. They had always been so close that in her great loneliness she must have rejoiced to follow him so shortly. She died at the early age of thirty-six leaving unfinished the work she had just begun for her fellow Jews.

"THOU ART OUR BROTHER"

In the summer of 1882, when the Russian immigration was at its height, an article appeared in "The Jewish Messenger." It concluded: "May our cultured men and women find no nobler field for their culture than personally lending hand and heart to the cause, saying to the downtrodden Russian: Come thou with us; thou art our brother; thou shalt learn many things of us; we shall learn much of thee."

Except for the humble admission in the last sentence this appeal neatly expresses the attitude of the majority of the German Jews of the United States. They had already organized committees and collected money for the immediate needs of the Russian immigrants. They hoped to find employment for the newcomers, to educate and Americanize these uprooted and bewildered "brothers."

But the Russians didn't want to be anybody's brother! Who

wants to be patronized by a prosperous, older relative even if his assistance is badly needed? Nearly all the Russian Jews came to this country desperately poor; they resented the help they must receive at least for a little while from these haughty Germans.

The majority of the German Jews prided themselves on their Americanism. A few of their group, they conceded, might still speak English with an accent; but wasn't that better than not being able to speak English at all? They felt that the Yiddish the Russians used was uncouth and barbarous. The children of the earlier German immigration managed to forget that their own ancestors had originated Yiddish, a language largely composed of German and written in Hebrew.

The Russians in self-defense called the protesting German brothers uneducated because of their ignorance of Hebrew. A child of six in Eastern Europe, ran their boast, knew more of the holy tongue than the president of many a Reform Temple in America. As for Yiddish—well, it was the "mother-language" of the Russian Jew and he would continue to love it even in America. Let the Germans beware! In just a few years, boasted the newcomers, we will have our own Yiddish newspapers and theaters.

There was also a cleavage in religion. Not all the German Jews in the United States had accepted Reform. Now the number of those who remained Orthodox was greatly increased by the ultra-Orthodox Russians. But many of the latter refused to do as the Germans had done before them and join an already existing synagogue. They thought that even the Germans who considered themselves strictly Orthodox were too lax in their religious observances. Besides, it was much more congenial for a group who had come from the same neighborhood in Europe to establish a Roumanian or Lithuanian synagogue for worship and study of the Torah.

Unlike the German group, the Russian showed extremely violent contrasts. On one side were these ultra-Orthodox; they had little interest in secular education except for their children, or in politics for they were strong in their belief that it was better to depend on God than on any earthly government. In the opposite camp gathered the rebels who had grown up under Czarist tyranny. Many of them had little or no devotion to their ancestral faith. In Russia they had rebelled against their oppressive government by joining non-Jewish radicals who had formed Anarchist or Socialist groups. These restless, idealistic refugees from the injustice of the Czar did much to build up the Labor movement in America.

207

As soon as the Russians began to arrive in overwhelming numbers in the United States, attempts were made to distribute them throughout the country. But the majority of them preferred to live near friends and relatives already settled in the larger cities of the East, especially New York. Some earned a living as carpenters, cigar makers or tailors. Some became peddlers or small shop keepers as they had once been in Europe.

The needlework trade absorbed many of the newcomers long before they could speak English. It seemed a blessing that a "greenhorn" could find a job as soon as he got off the boat! At first the Russian immigrants rejoiced to receive such high wages; they must have seemed princely compared to the sum paid for a week's work back home. But it did not take the newcomers long to learn how money melted away in America.

For a while the bewildered strangers were too frightened to protest against their inadequate wage and the inhumanly long hours they sat bent over their machines in the ill-ventilated factories. At this period the sweatshop was one of the most horrible features of the garment trade. A workman whose earnings could not be stretched to support his family eagerly accepted clothing to be sewed at home. For what sometimes amounted to a few dollars a week his wife and the half-grown children would work together in the dingy tenement kitchen which often served as living and bedroom as well as home-factory. Yes, and lodging house also! For in order to pay the rent many an immigrant took in roomers.

Because so many of the "sweated workers" were Jews it seems fitting that one of the most successful agitators for the rights of labor should have been of Jewish birth.

Samuel Gompers had been a worker from his boyhood in London, where his father, a cigar maker, taught the boy his trade. When Samuel was still a child the family came to New York. The fourteen-year-old boy was too poor to go to school and managed to find work as a cigar maker. He hated the job—the everlasting rolling of the strong smelling tobacco; the foul air of the over-crowded room. Sometimes he wondered bitterly whether he would be obliged to spend the rest of his life in a crowded, stuffy loft, rolling the acrid tobacco through the tedious, empty hours.

Interior of an Improved Sweat Shop

There was only one break in the dreadful monotony. Often while the others rolled their endless brown bundles, a worker would read to them for an hour from a newspaper or magazine. As the workers were paid according to the number of cigars they turned out in a day, each paid the reader with cigars that he might not fall behind in his earnings. The cigar makers soon preferred young Gompers' reading; they insisted the youth from London should not go back to his work table at the end of the hour. So Gompers read on and on, a task he found much more enjoyable than rolling cigars.

Now he began to attend evening classes at Cooper Union, that university for poor, ambitious boys on New York's East Side. Whenever Samuel Gompers had the opportunity he listened to lectures; he became interested in public speaking and began to take part in debates. When he returned home from night school his head swam and his eyes drooped from weariness, but he forced himself to keep awake to read the library books several envied fellow-workers with good educations had advised him to study.

He became interested in labor conditions and the unions which the workers in various trades had formed to protect themselves from unfair treatment. When the underpaid cigar makers formed their own union young Samuel Gompers became its president.

The first labor unions in the United States had been declared illegal. In Gompers' time many unions were still fighting to keep alive. Samuel Gompers urged that instead of fighting as individual groups for better wages and working conditions for their members, these unions should form one large body which would be able to improve labor conditions all over the United States. He was one of the founders of the powerful American Federation of Labor and in 1886 became its first president, an office he was to hold for over forty years.

Gompers seems to have had little interest in Judaism, but in striving for the justice which was sought centuries ago by our prophets he fulfilled their loftiest ideals and brought honor to the Jewish people.

As we look back over the years we may be proud as Jews of the contributions of Gompers and other Jewish leaders to the cause of labor. Some of them greatly improved the relations between the employer and the men he hired by introducing arbitration and an industrial court. Organizations like the International Ladies Garment Workers' Union in which Jewish workers predominate have been leaders in providing unemployment insurance, summer camps and medical care for their members.

Gompers was an old man but still vigorous and far-sighted when during the First World War he was called to serve as a member of the Committee of National Defense. As in every other war the government needed the cooperation of every worker behind the lines; Gompers did his best to see that every working man in the United States offered his cooperation.

211

After the war he accepted the invitation of President Woodrow Wilson to go to France for the signing of the Peace Treaty. Here he was honored by labor leaders from many European countries; later he was asked to serve on a committee to make new and better labor laws for all the governments of the world.

A JEWISH EXPLORER

Have you noticed how often in this history it has been easy to tell the story of the growth of a movement in conjunction with the life of one of its leaders? Earlier we sketched the careers of two leaders of Reform and Orthodox Judaism. Now a word about the group known as Conservative and one of the ablest of its representatives, Dr. Solomon Schechter.

The Conservative Synagogue has never been ready to adopt all the changes favored by the Reform group. On the other hand, it believes in change and has accepted a good many innovations still rejected by the Orthodox, such as Confirmation for both girls and boys and the family pew.

The center of this movement may be said to be the Jewish Theological Seminary in New York City. This school for the training of rabbis and teachers was established in 1886. It is worth noting that at the turn of the century when the project seemed about to fail for lack of funds, Jews of the Reform group like the famous lawyer, Louis Marshall, helped to raise money for its support. For by 1901 the violence of the days of Isaac M. Wise was happily forgotten, or at least forgiven.

This was the year when a new president for the Jewish Theological Seminary came to New York.

Solomon Schechter was born in a small town in Roumania in 1850. His Jewish knowledge and his studies in Vienna recommended him to a post at Cambridge University in England. Here the great adventure of his life began. Strictly speaking, it was not a Jewish adventure in America. But because we like the story so much and the fame Dr. Schechter won through his discoveries in the Genizah may have had something to do with his coming to this country, we insist on telling it here and now.

But what is a Genizah? It is a storehouse for badly torn Hebrew books and Scrolls of the Torah. Since the Jew is forbidden to destroy even a scrap of parchment on which the holy tongue is written, they are buried or hidden away in some safe and secret place. Next, what is the Apocrypha? This name is given to the group of ancient books which for various reasons were not included in the authorized version of our Bible. Having delayed you with two really necessary definitions, we'll hurry on to Solomon Schechter's great discovery.

The Book of Ben Sira, one of the works included in the Apocrypha, was originally written in Hebrew. But for centuries scholars could find only the Greek translation. Then in 1896 two English women who had been traveling in the Near East brought home with them a few fragments of papyrus covered with Hebrew writing. Would the great scholar, Dr. Schechter, please tell them what the writing meant?

From the century-dimmed words Dr. Schechter managed to reconstruct a passage of the lost manuscript. As soon as he could he left for Egypt, where, in the ancient synagogue at Cairo, he began his search through the Genizah. Here in the choking dust and twilight dimness he unearthed thousands of Hebrew manuscripts, some almost complete, while of others only a few tattered fragments remained. He did not search in vain; among the torn pieces of papyrus he found the precious writings of Ben Sira—in Hebrew.

This discovery was of the greatest value to Hebrew scholars all over the world. Dr. Schechter might have spent the rest of his life studying the manuscripts he brought home to England and discussing their contents in his scholarly books. But when he received the call to become the president of the recently organized Jewish Theological Seminary, he felt it was his duty to come to America. In New York he continued to write and lecture as well as to fill the position of head of the Seminary and the teacher of future Conservative rabbis.

His monument today is not only this important institution with its ever increasing list of graduates. Among other assets the Seminary boasts the greatest Jewish library in the world and an impressive Jewish Museum. Its weekly radio program, the "Eternal Light," does much to increase the knowledge not only of Jews but of Gentiles who wish to learn more about Judaism.

THE FIRST WORLD WAR

The Spanish-American War of 1898 was mercifully short and drew such small forces into its service that it had little or no effect on our Jewish citizens. The Jews who fought in it were in honorable proportion to the nation's population; our Jewish soldiers conducted themselves in a way to reflect credit on every Jewish citizen; their merit was rewarded by the high rank they attained in both the army and navy, while Jewish admirers of Theodore Roosevelt rejoiced to learn that at least six Jews fought in his picturesque "Rough Riders."

But the First World War was fought on a far more stupendous scale. One historian has estimated that the Jews listed in the American army, navy and marine corps during that struggle outnumber the entire Jewish population in the United States in 1861. Again we could name many high ranking officers, list the official citations of Jewish soldiers who received such high honors as the Distinguished Service Cross, the Croix de Guerre and the rarely awarded Congressional Medal of Honor.

COMPARISON OF UNITED STATES
AND JEWISH SOLDIERS, SAILORS
AND MARINES IN FOUR WARS

UNITED STATES ARMED FORCES

JEWISH SOLDIERS, SAILORS AND MARINES

15,513,657

4,057,101

2,128,948

280,564

| 6,000 JEWS | 4,000 JEWS | 200,000 JEWS | 550,000 JEWS |
| CIVIL WAR | SPANISH-AMERICAN WAR | 1st WORLD WAR | 2nd WORLD WAR |

The war records of these heroes are as thrilling as any tale of old time chivalry. But instead of telling their stories, perhaps it might be better to mention several rather significant innovations.

You may remember that during the Civil War the Jews after a protest secured governmental recognition of their chaplains. Now with a vastly greater number of Jewish men bearing arms, many more Jewish chaplains were needed. Instead of the three rabbis who acted as chaplains in the Civil War, twenty-five were commissioned in 1918. Twelve served in France, one in the navy, while the others carried on their work in camps in the United States.

There were also civilian workers sent to France and to the home camps by the newly established Jewish Welfare Board. This organization aided greatly in keeping up the morale of soldiers of all faiths who visited their various centers both in this country and abroad. The JWB, as it soon came to be called, was especially useful in providing prayer books for miiltary services as well as wine and matzoth for the Passover. Its representatives like the Red Cross visited the sick and wounded in hospitals and arranged for entertainments and home hospitality for service men on leave. This Board earned the gratitude of many sorrowing families by cooperating with the government to place the traditional Magen David instead of the cross above the graves of Jews who were buried in military cemeteries.

This war, like every other, carried in its wake other trage-dies besides crushed limbs and blinded eyes and flag-covered coffins. Now the American citizens faced not only epidemics and unemployment but newly awakened prejudices and dis-trust of those who might differ from the majority in color or the country of their birth or religion.

After the Civil War the Negro in the South had been the chief victim of the fantastic secret organization known and feared as the Ku Klux Klan. After the First World War the Klan revived with its maskings and floggings and its fiery cross. But now the sheeted riders rode in the North as well as the South; the objects of their persecution were not only Negroes but also Catholics, foreigners and Jews.

There were other organizations, some mercifully short-lived, and others which for years managed to create hatred and mis-trust between American and American. There was the hate-campaign of the multi-millionaire Henry Ford. A favorite slander of the anti-Semites of this period ran that Jewish sol-diers had all held easy and safe jobs; that "you never saw a Jewish grave in France." The Magen Davids in every American war cemetery abroad gave the lie to such accusations. But what proof ever convinced a fanatic?

As early as 1906 three American Jewish leaders, Louis Marshall, Dr. Cyrus Adler and Jacob Schiff had organized the

American Jewish Committee. We have already mentioned one of the Bnai Brith's most important projects, the Anti-Defamation League. Now in 1917, due largely to the inspiration of Rabbi Stephen S. Wise, the American Jewish Congress was organized for Jewish self-defense.

One result of the war, then, was an increase of anti-Semitism; this helped to create a new unity among American Jews who felt that they must join forces if they hoped to withstand slanderous attacks. A far greater crisis had already drawn the Jews of the United States together: Jewish war relief.

There had been dreadful suffering throughout war-torn Europe. But the Jews of Russia and adjoining countries suffered the most. Many of the unfortunates lived in the path of the invading German armies. In certain areas the Russian and the German troops advanced and retreated six times over towns which they had turned into a battlefield.

The inhabitants who escaped often died of starvation and exposure on the roads. Even when they reached a haven, the war made it impossible for charitable European Jews to provide adequate shelter and food and clothing for the refugees. But the Jews of rich America were still untouched by the war! The Joint Distribution Committee was formed to care for the survivors, especially the war orphans. In aiding these unfortunates across the sea the Jews of America grew closer to each other for they realized as never before that all Israel are brothers.

THE BEGINNING OF ZIONISM IN AMERICA

There was another unifying force between American Jews which the First World War did much to develop and strengthen —Zionism, although at the beginning it divided rather than united American Jewry.

You may recall how some years after the failure of his generous dream, Mordecai Noah became interested in the return of persecuted and homeless Jews to Palestine. Emma Lazarus, even as she wrote of the sufferings of her people, wondered whether their ancient Homeland might be the answer. These two very different Jews have sometimes been called our earliest American Zionists. But there were others and we intend to tell you about one of them.

When some of the 1880 Russian refugees settled in Baltimore, they found two understanding friends in Rabbi Benjamin Szold and his oldest daughter, Henrietta. It is a great temptation to stop and chat with the rabbi's daughter, a slender, straight-shouldered woman with keen eyes and a rather stubborn chin. But we will meet her again; so it may be better to listen to the Russian guests gathered around the Szold dinner table. They interrupt each other in their eagerness. Many young Russians, they say, have formed societies which are dedicated to the restoration of Palestine. What a pity, one of the immigrants declares, that there are no such societies in America!

Later Henrietta Szold joined a group of Baltimore enthusiasts in what is believed to have been the first Zionist organization in the United States.

In 1897 the First Zionist Congress met in Basle. The delegates had been summoned to Switzerland by an Austrian journalist, Theodor Herzl, the author of *The Jewish State*. His plan to secure Palestine as a permanent home for his long dispersed people resounded like a battle cry throughout Europe.

Here in the United States the birth of Zionism was greeted with enthusiasm or contempt or indifference. Many who considered themselves loyal Jews were too busy supporting their own institutions to take part in what they considered an impractical and visionary scheme. Curiously enough, two of the groups which bitterly opposed the Zionist movement were the widely apart ultra-Orthodox Russian and the Reform German Jews.

The former was sincere in his prayers for a return to Zion; but, he insisted, this would be brought about by a miracle of God's choice and it was impious to depend on human efforts. The Jews of German birth, and especially their American-born children, followed the teaching of the first Reform rabbis: Judaism was a religion and those who followed it were not a nation. The Jews of the United States, they affirmed, were Americans; only their ancestral faith bound them to Jews in other countries. They believed that to take part in any movement to reestablish the Jews as a separate nation on their own land was disloyal to the country in which the Jew had found his home.

So when after the first Congress at Basle Jewish American leaders like Rabbi Stephen S. Wise and Professor Richard Gottheil became officers in a newly founded American Federation of Zionists, many of their friends were surprised and shocked. Just as Miss Szold's one hundred per cent. American friends in Baltimore had been shocked when she had joined the pioneer group.

HENRIETTA SZOLD, LADY WITH A MISSION

Henrietta Szold had already served her people as writer and teacher and as the first secretary of the Jewish Publication Society. When in 1909 she became ill as a result of overwork, the board of the Society rewarded her long and faithful services with a trip to Europe and the Near East.

She returned from Palestine with the one burning desire which was to dominate her life and to strengthen greatly the growth of Zionism in the United States. Henrietta Szold told her friends of horrible sights neither she nor they could ever forget: the squalor and poverty of the Jews of Palestine; the lack of hospitals; children whose eyesight might easily have been saved by modern doctors.

In New York City a dozen Jewish women met with Miss Szold and formed the first chapter of Hadassah. The charter members chose the Hebrew name of Queen Esther for their group as they had organized on the Feast of Purim. The quotation from Jeremiah on their seal expressed their purpose: "For the Healing of the Daughter of my People."

In time chapters were formed in city after city from New York to San Francisco. Few women could resist the appeal to aid the helpless sick of Palestine. Many who were not interested in political Zionism were eager to contribute funds to build sadly needed health centers or to furnish milk to undernourished school children.

When the First World War broke out Palestine still suffered from the misrule of the Turks. The war brought added privation and disease. Under the leadership of Miss Szold, national president of Hadassah, funds were raised to equip and send a medical unit to Palestine. Large sums were contributed by the Zionists of America and the Joint Distribution Committee. The forty-four doctors and trained nurses of the unit wore a red Magen David on the sleeves of their khaki uniforms.

Before the group reached Jerusalem they were overjoyed to hear that the Turkish armies were retreating before the English forces, for Great Britain in the Balfour Declaration had already promised to protect and to help establish a "national home" in Palestine for Jews from all over the world.

Henrietta Szold spent the last twenty-three years of her life in Palestine, where she devoted her fine executive talent to health work, education and social service, but she never lost touch with her native country. In her frequent visits home she inspired thousands of American women with her stories of the devotion and the heroism of the Jewish pioneers. Her followers tried to show their love for her with costly gifts, but she wanted nothing for herself; she only asked for unbelievably huge sums, each larger than the last, to help her carry on her chosen mission.

ANOTHER FIGHTING RABBI, STEPHEN S. WISE

Around the time of the First World War three very different Jews were drawn together by their pity for the distressed and their love for Palestine. Three giants of yesterday, so unlike in background and character, so alike in their devotion to their people: Rabbi Stephen S. Wise, Justice Louis D. Brandeis and Nathan Straus.

Again we meet a rabbi who for years stood in the foremost rank of Americans as organizer and fighter for what he believed to be the truth. This modern prophet, Stephen S. Wise, was born in Hungary in 1874. When the boy was still an infant,

The Three Giants (Nathan Straus, Louis D. Brandeis, Stephen S. Wise)

his father came to the United States, where he successfully occupied pulpits in Brooklyn and New York City.

As a young man Stephen Wise served as rabbi in New York City and Portland, Oregon. By his early thirties he had gained such a reputation as an orator that he was offered the pulpit of one of the most important congregations in the East. But he felt he could not accept this tempting offer unless he received the congregation's promise that he would be allowed to express his own personal views from the pulpit. This was refused and Rabbi Stephen Wise decided it was time for him to create his own congregation where he would enjoy unlimited freedom to express his often radical ideas.

In New York City in 1907 he founded the Free Synagogue, the most liberal Jewish institution of that day. Many timid souls thought he was far too daring in his efforts to improve

225

social conditions, for he did more than repeat the passionate appeals of Israel's prophets for justice. In his own life he followed their example by defending every liberal cause.

Many of these causes have long since been won; changes for which Rabbi Wise and other liberals of his day fought so fearlessly are now taken for granted. He defended the suffrage movement when to approve of Votes for Women made the defender a target of abuse or at least ridicule. We have already mentioned the part he played in establishing the Zionist Organization of America at a time when very, very few rabbis of the Reform wing to which he belonged were ready to agree with him. He had the courage to join a group which attacked corrupt politics in New York City and forced the mayor to resign. The warrior-rabbi was always ready to defend the rights of labor; once he risked his position by refusing the demand of his congregation that he remain silent during the long and terrible steel strike.

Although Stephen Wise was famous for his oratory in Jewish and Gentile circles all over the United States, he knew that swaying audiences by his eloquence was not enough. No one realized more keenly than he that the synagogue was no longer the center of Jewish life. Its care for the stranger, the orphan and the aged had been taken over by various charitable groups. To supplement this aid and unite it more closely to Jewish life, Rabbi Wise introduced social service as part of the program of his Free Synagogue. One of its most successful projects, the adoption of Jewish children, was introduced by the rabbi's artist-wife, Louise Waterman Wise.

During the First World War Rabbi Wise was constantly in demand as a speaker at patriotic meetings. To dramatize the need for workers in war industries, the orator worked by the side of his son James in a shipyard. When peace came, it was Rabbi Wise's authority as a two-term president of the Zionist Organization of America and his strong friendship with President Wilson that helped him win certain concessions for Palestine at Versailles.

Later Rabbi Wise, who felt there should be a liberal training school for rabbis in a great Jewish center like New York, founded the Jewish Institute of Religion. Today, as we have already noted, this institution is united with the older Hebrew Union College. One of his most impressive contributions to Jewish unity was the organization of a World Jewish Congress in 1936; this Congress was made up of representatives of Jews from twenty-six nations. Rabbi Wise was already president of the American Jewish Congress formed for the protection of Jewish rights in Palestine and Europe. Now he was honored with the presidency of this new world-wide organization.

He lived to see the persecution of Hitler which doomed six million Jews to death; he lived through the doubts and fears of a Second World War. Heartsick but undaunted, he still fought as valiantly although perhaps not as hopefully as in his youth.

Stephen S. Wise died at the age of seventy-five, if one may be said to die, when so many splendid memorials live on to do him honor.

BRANDEIS OF THE SUPREME COURT

The second of our trio of modern giants was also the son of immigrants. Early in the German mass migration of 1848, Joseph Brandeis, who had wearied of Austrian oppression, left his native Bohemia for America. The girl he expected to marry joined a group of distinguished intellectuals who the same year followed him to freedom. Their child, Louis D. Brandeis, won the honor of being the first Jew to serve on the Supreme Court of the United States.

When Brandeis practised law, first in St. Louis, then in Boston, he won a lesser but most significant honor, the title of "the people's lawyer," for he defended the common man against unfair working conditions, and furthered fairer taxation and insurance laws. As the friend of labor he earned the enmity of "big business" interests like the railroads, which later opposed his appointment to the Supreme Court. His brilliant record there made it easier for two other Jewish lawyers, Benjamin N. Cardozo and Felix Frankfurter, to follow him.

As a young man Brandeis had shown little interest in Jewish

affairs. But little by little his imagination was fired by the romance of Zionism; his interest in the movement drew him, as it had drawn many other indifferent American Jews, into a whirlpool of Jewish activity. In 1914 leadership in Zionist work shifted from war-torn Europe to the still neutral United States. In such troubled times the Provisional Executive Committee for Zionist Affairs needed a man with a strong hand and a cool head for its chairman, and Louis D. Brandeis took over.

As a member of the Supreme Court Justice Brandeis found it necessary to sever all official connections with Zionism. But his appointment to the highest court in the land aided the movement far more than continued years of active service might have done. Many Jews had long protested that a loyal American could never be a Zionist. President Wilson by his appointment made clear what he thought of such a statement.

SAFE MILK FOR BABIES

The last of our trio must serve as a picture of an ideal Jewish philanthropist, who in a larger and more troubled day carried out his benefactions in the spirit of Judah Touro. There have been many wealthy and generous Jews in the United States since Touro's day; to mention but two out of a possible twenty, what about Julian Rosenwald, with his deep interest in Negro education; and Jacob H. Schiff, who in his love for Jewish learning financed the Semitic department of New York City's Public Library and founded the Semitic Museum at Harvard University?

But for our ideal modern philanthropist we choose Nathan Straus. He was born in Talbotton, Georgia, in 1848, the son of a German-born shopkeeper, whose family were to own and operate Macy's department store in New York City. One son, Isidor, is remembered as one of the founders and later the president of the Educational Alliance of New York, an institution which did much for the Americanization of the immigrant. Another son, Oscar, was three times Minister to Turkey and Secretary of Commerce and Labor, the first American Jew to serve as a member of the president's cabinet. And to make an already famous family even more famous, there was the youngest son, Nathan Straus!

He was an able business man, but he seemed glad to retire that he might devote all of his time to his hobby—philanthropy. The most famous of his many philanthropies, which saved the lives of many thousands of babies and has helped to preserve the health of children of our own day, was the Straus Milk Fund. The story of its origin has been told many times, but it is well worth repeating.

In 1892 dairies lacked adequate inspection. Milk often became infected and brought sickness and even death to those who drank it. Nathan Straus lived with his family on his

230

country estate; he prided himself on his fine herd of cattle. A cow that had seemed perfectly healthy suddenly died—from tuberculosis. What a lucky escape for the Straus children. Their father vowed that he would have his milk herd watched even more closely. And what about the recent discoveries of Louis Pasteur? Hadn't the French scientist demonstrated that the germs in milk become absolutely harmless when treated by the Pasteur method?

Yes, decided Mr. Straus, after this every one in my family will drink pasteurized milk.

But although his own child might be safe, Mr. Straus insisted on worrying about other people's children. He knew that in the hot weather New York tenement babies often died like flies—after drinking contaminated milk. At last he hit on what seemed to him to be a practical and simple plan. Pasteurize all milk and make it safe to drink!

Mr. Straus learned that his plan wasn't so very simple after all. The dairy owners objected violently to the expense of equipping their plant with pasteurizing machines. If they did so, they warned, they would have to raise the price of milk.

231

The customers grumbled that they were already overcharged. Some asked bitterly whether Mr. Straus had started this foolish fuss over perfectly good milk just to make it more expensive, that he might share the added profits with the dairies.

The millionaire didn't worry over such silly insults. But he did worry about the silly people who refused to accept a new idea. They would have to be educated! So he spent a fortune opening stations in the poorer sections of New York where pasteurized milk was sold for a few pennies a quart; those unable to pay received it free.

Meanwhile Mr. Straus began his great campaign for adequate milk inspection by the state. Years passed but at last he was able to close his private pasteurization laboratory, for in every state in the union pasteurization finally became a law.

It was not enough for our philanthropist that the children of America had safe milk. After a visit to Palestine he established a pasteurization plant there along with soup kitchens and health centers. Nathan Straus had in the early days provided funds to pay the passage of the first two Hadassah nurses who brought hope and healing to Palestine. He and his equally generous wife, Lina Straus, who had sold her jewels to aid the Homeland, believed that the work must go on.

He gave large sums for the relief of those who suffered from the First World War. His death spared him the knowledge of the horrors of the Hitler persecution and of another conflict, even more terrible than the last.

232

Jewish Internees

AMERICAN JEWS TO THE RESCUE

After their defeat in World War I, the Germans settled down to an uneasy peace. They were crushed beneath the load of an intolerable war debt; they suffered from a business depression and nation-wide unemployment, but even more from shame over their defeat. It was easy for them to believe the ambitious little corporal, Adolph Hitler, when he told them that not the allied armies but treacherous German Jews had brought about Germany's defeat.

Hitler shouted that there was but one remedy for the misfortunes which tormented Germany—the Jews must be wiped out. The mob which believed all the vicious lies of the Hitlerian party screamed back a frenzied Yes!

At first there were boycotts of Jewish firms, often accompanied by violence. Then came the yellow badge which every Jew was forced to wear; it marked him as a declassed citizen, who was not permitted to attend the theater or occupy any but a few restricted benches in the public parks. Jewish school children were assigned to segregated desks; not only their classmates but their teachers jeered at and tormented them.

How to save these children? Again the American Jews played their part. The National Council of Jewish Women, which since its beginnings in 1892 had worked with immigrants, now arranged for German parents to send their children to this country. Here they were cared for until their parents could also emigrate; when orphaned through the unspeakable cruelties of Hitler and his Nazis they were often adopted by their American protectors.

Child rescue on a far larger scale was begun by our old friend, Henrietta Szold, in 1933. She had decided to retire and spend her last years in America, but now with the aid of a few German Jews she organized the Youth Aliyah, named after the pilgrimages to ancient Jerusalem. On its twentieth anniversary this organization claimed that it had rescued sixty-five thousand children to live useful, normal lives in Palestine. This work of mercy, a major project of Hadassah, was another strong link between the New Land of the Jew and the Old.

In a history as short as this it is really impossible even to list the many organizations of American women who have worked for Israel. But when we speak of Youth Aliyah we

234

should remember the splendid work carried on by Women's American Ort, the group which by establishing schools for Jewish boys and girls in various countries educates them to live and work in Israel.

During the terrible days of the Hitler persecution, the American Jews did more than collect money for the victims and to bring as many as possible to our country. They tried to refute the Hitler propaganda which was often repeated by anti-Semitic groups; they organized mass meetings to protect against German injustice; some urged a boycott to impress upon the German people the indignation of a civilized world. All efforts proved useless; six million Jews, not only those of German birth but countless victims from German-conquered territory, perished in cattle cars, in concentration camps and crematoria.

THE SECOND WORLD WAR

In the United States many an immigrant Jew who because of his recent arrival could not be drafted, volunteered to fight against the enemy not only of his people but all mankind. Again we have the picture of another World War with its stories of patriotic devotion by soldier and civilian, its heartbreak and its idealism. We will only point out that World War II covered far more territory than did its predecessor, and that the United States entered nearer the beginning of the conflict than in 1917, and supplied a vastly larger number of men in every branch of the service.

The Jews in the armed forces represented 11% of the entire Jewish population of the United States; their total number reaches the amazing figure of 550,000. Of these, 35,000 were listed as casualties, missing or taken prisoner, wounded or killed in action. Again Jews in camp and hospital desired their own chaplains. In this war three hundred and eleven ordained rabbis drawn from Orthodox, Conservative and Reform groups served the needs not only of Jewish youths but any young men who came to them for aid or advice.

Since 61,500 decorations were awarded to 35,000 Jewish combatants in the army, navy and air force, there are countless stories of almost unbelievable heroism. We will tell just one, the story of four chaplains, one of them a Jew.

FOUR CHAPLAINS

A Catholic priest, two Protestant ministers and a rabbi had all enlisted in the service and were on their way to their assignments in Greenland. Rabbi Alexander Goode had forced himself to leave his wife and young son, his congregation in York, Pennsylvania, his studies and his work for the community. Although a chaplain is rated as a non-combatant he knows when he enters the over-seas service that he will face hardships and many dangers. He cannot know his fate—he can only hope to meet it bravely.

The waters of the North Atlantic grew more and more turbulent on that February 3 of the year 1943. The cold bit through the coats and uniforms of the soldiers, but they felt secure in the safety of shipboard...

Suddenly a warning cry rose and silenced the soldiers' idle chatter. The ship had been struck by a torpedo; immediately it began to sink.

In the confusion terror-stricken soldiers shouted that they could not find their life-belts. One after the other the four chaplains unfastened their one hope of safety in the treacherous sea. We hear the muttered protest of the soldiers—Chap-

The Four Chaplains

lain, I can't take . . . The calm answer: You must! . . . Mumbled thanks; perhaps a handclasp for goodbye.

Waves covered the sagging deck where the four chaplains stood. The spray dashed over the uniformed shoulders, still straight with soldierly pride. But the heads of the four men were bent in prayer. Catholic, Protestants, Jew—each prayed to his own God in his own fashion but not for himself, only for the common humanity in which these men believed and for whose sake they died.

AFTER THE SECOND WORLD WAR

After the Second World War ended it was at last possible to aid many of Hitler's victims who could not be reached before. Again American Jews were united in their pity for the remnants of a sorely tried people rescued from the Nazi concentration camps; for the broken families long since driven from their homes and now emerging fearfully from their hiding places. There had never been such an appeal before. To give only a top figure: in 1948 the United Jewish Appeal, which included the Joint Distribution Committee and the Palestine Appeal, collected the stupendous sum of $150,000,000.

A large proportion of the uprooted Jews of Europe wished to emigrate to Palestine. Great Britain was still in control of that country and made drastic efforts to curtail immigration there. Some American boys volunteered to serve on the ships which tried to run the British blockade and bring the illegal immigrants into harbor. The British finally withdrew in 1948 and Palestine, declaring its independence, became the State of Israel. A number of veterans of World War II had enrolled at the Hebrew University. In the war with the Arabs which followed many of these American students fought in the ranks by the side of their Israeli comrades.

The long and heroic struggle to rebuild the Homeland did much to strengthen Zionism in the United States. Even those who had been lukewarm in their desire for a Jewish state recognized the need for a haven for the Jews who had survived Hitler's cruelty. American Jews thrilled with pride when returning tourists told of the country's progress. It is hardly too much to say that today practically every Jew in the United States is an active worker for Israel, or at least sympathetic to its interests.

Love for Israel is still a strong tie to bind together the many different types of Jews we have in our country today. A time will come when that brave little state's many immigrants will be able to support not only themselves but Israel's many splendid institutions. But when the need for fund raising for Jews outside of America disappears what bond will remain to unite us? For a while it may be necessary to support our own defense organizations against anti-Semitism. It is hoped that these defense groups will gradually broaden the work they

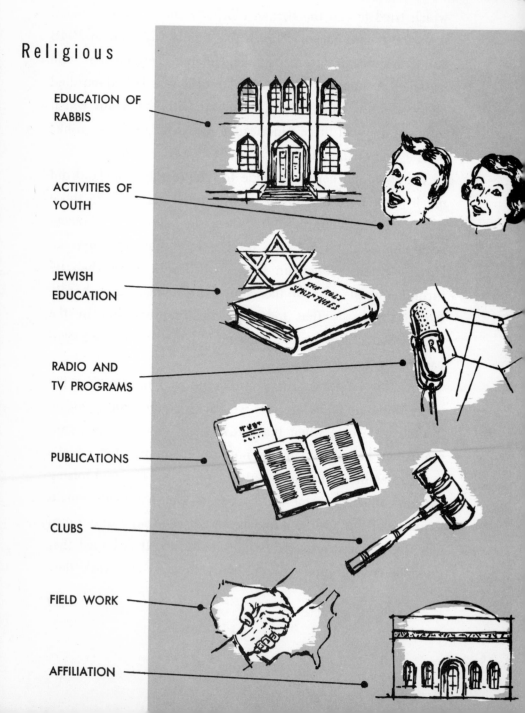

Religious

EDUCATION OF
RABBIS

ACTIVITIES OF
YOUTH

JEWISH
EDUCATION

RADIO AND
TV PROGRAMS

PUBLICATIONS

CLUBS

FIELD WORK

AFFILIATION

ERVICES OF NATIONAL JEWISH ORGANIZATIONS

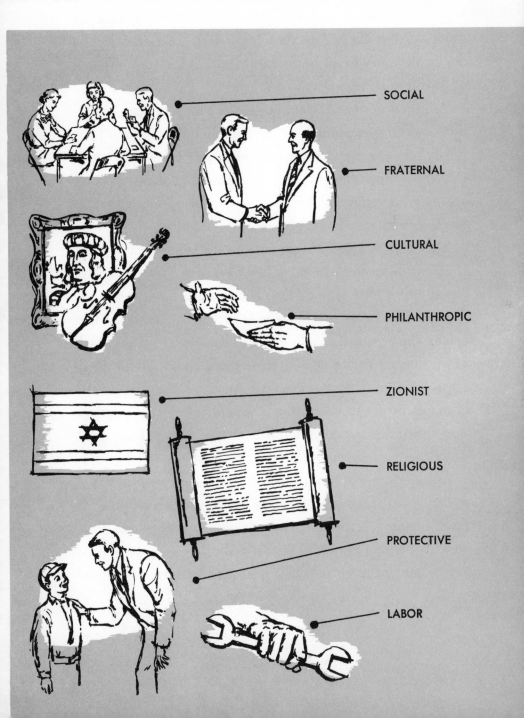

SOCIAL

FRATERNAL

CULTURAL

PHILANTHROPIC

ZIONIST

RELIGIOUS

PROTECTIVE

LABOR

have already begun—to protest not only against discrimination toward the Jew, but against the Negro and other minority groups. When every American Jew realizes that an injury to one is an injury to all he will learn at last the true meaning of American Democracy.

As Americans we will continue to work for American institutions and American ideals; as Jews we will unite to support our synagogue, our welfare organizations, our schools. Yeshiva University with its new Medical School and Brandeis University are only a beginning. We have accomplished much, but so much remains to be accomplished.

This story of Jewish Adventures in the United States is far from complete. For one thing, we have not given the names of any living Jews, who by their achievement have paid something of the debt our people owe America. If we gave Einstein among the scientists, Ludwig Lewisohn among writers, Jack Levine among artists, and—but we could go on and on. Mere lists of the great ones among our American Jews have little meaning. So let us study their accomplishments in lengthier works than this and be grateful that we may claim these great Americans for our people.

As you close this book, you may wonder why we have said so little of the conditions that face the Jew in America exactly three hundred years after the refugees arrived in the little Dutch village on the banks of the Hudson.

The present is so close that it is hard to judge wisely and

to set down the correct conclusions. A moment ago we told of our hopes for a peaceful world. But even as we wrote we thought of certain young Jews who will never return from their adventure in Korea. We spoke of Israel, strong and self sufficient, but it is impossible to ignore the almost daily border skirmishes which may result in a long and bloody conflict in the Near East. We cannot prophesy—we can only hope.

Sometimes we wonder whether a history like this should be bound between the covers of a volume. Wouldn't it be safer to keep our record in a loose-leaf notebook? Then year by year we might add the stirring and undreamed of events which the future will dictate to the historian of tomorrow.

But anyone who has studied the Adventures of the Jew in America may say with certainty:

We are today five million strong—the largest and richest and most influential Jewish community in the whole world. As Jews we are bound together by our religion, our work for our unfortunates, our defense against anti-Semitism. For three hundred years the Jew has walked with courage and dignity in the first country in the whole world to grant him the rights of citizenship. In the past we have shown our love and gratitude to America in many ways; we will be no less grateful in the future.

Los Altos, Calif.
1954

INDEX

Valley Forge, 57
Virginia, 38

War of 1812, 111
Washington, George, 53, 63, 100;
    and Jewish congregations, 71f
West India Company, 13f
West Indies, 39
Williams, Roger, 22
Williamson, Major Andrew,
    Salvador's commander, 52-4
Wilson, Woodrow, and Gompers,
    212; appointment of Brandeis,
    229; friend of S. S. Wise, 227
Wise, Isaac Mayer, 148, 150-1,
    152, 188f; Paducah case, 174-5

Wise, Louise Waterman, 227
Wise, Stephen, S., 224f; American
    Jewish Congress, 219; American
    Federation of Zionists, 222
Women's American Ort, 235
World Jewish Congress, 227
World War I, 215-6
World War II, 227, 235f

Yeshiva University, 242
Yiddish, 206
Youth Aliyah, 234
Yulee (Levy), David, Florida
    senator, 159f

Zionism, 239; in America, 220f

JEWISH ADVENTURES IN AMERICA

Elma Ehrlich Levinger

In writing this volume the author, nationally known for her numerous books and plays for children and adults, has followed a unique approach. She presents her story, wherever possible, through the biographies of Jewish men and women who have played some part in creating Jewish history in America.

Between the stories of her heroes and heroines, Mrs. Levinger has presented the necessary background of events in vivid and popular style. It reads at times like fiction but in every instance the author has carefully documented her facts.

(*Continued on back flap*)

Book and jacket designed by William Steinel

Jewish Adventures in America is the history of the Jews in America from the time when New York was still New Amsterdam, up to the year 1954-55, when American Jews celebrate the three hundredth anniversary of the arrival of a little band of refugees.

Though in a volume of this size it is impossible to tell the whole fascinating story, the author succeeded in her masterly story telling in high lighting her narrative with the biographies of certain Jews whose lives and pioneering deeds forged the pattern of American Jewry as part of the Great Adventures of American Life.

The book is divided into three parts:

I. We Come to America

II. We Grow With America

III. We Pay Our Debt to America

BLOCH PUBLISHING CO.

31 WEST 31st STREET
NEW YORK 1, N. Y.